Reporting Sexual Violence and #MeToo in Asia

This book provides a comprehensive analysis of the role of news media and social media in the propagation and treatment of the global #MeToo movement.

This comparative study uniquely spans Hong Kong, Taiwan, and mainland China—three culturally similar yet legally and politically distinct societies—to elucidate the variations in media systems in each society and the influence these differences bear on the role and impact of news media on social movements and rape culture. The author examines how journalistic coverage of rape cases and #MeToo has shaped public discourse, contributed to cyber activism, and influenced the strategies adopted by activists in these contexts, illuminating the complexities of news production processes, the influence of cultural contexts on media narratives, and the power of social media discourse. Taking into account the journalistic constraints and challenges in reporting sexual violence, effective strategies for public engagement and action are discussed alongside the potential for platforms to serve as support networks for survivors, proffering solutions for more effective and supportive reporting of sexual violence.

Offering invaluable new insights into the relationship between news media and sexual violence, this book is recommended reading for advanced students and researchers of media, gender, and social change.

Luwei Rose Luqiu is an Associate Professor for the School of Communication at Hong Kong Baptist University.

Routledge Focus on Journalism Studies

Election Politics and the Mass Press in Long Edwardian Britain
Christopher Shoop-Worrall

Peripheral Actors in Journalism
Deviating from the Norm?
Aljosha Karim Schapals

Journalism's Racial Reckoning
The News Media's Pivot to Diversity and Inclusion
Brad Clark

Re-examining the UK Newspaper Industry
Marc Edge

Undercover Reporting, Deception, and Betrayal in Journalism
Denis Muller and Andrea Carson

Nonverbal Neutrality of Broadcasters Covering Crisis
Not Just What You Say But How You Say It
Danielle Deavours

Evaluating Digital Sources in Journalism
Introduction to Digital Source Criticism
Ståle Grut

Reporting Sexual Violence and #MeToo in Asia
The View from Hong Kong, Mainland China, and Taiwan
Luwei Rose Luqiu

For more information about this series, please visit: https://www.routledge.com/Routledge-Focus-on-Journalism-Studies/book-series/RFJS

Reporting Sexual Violence and #MeToo in Asia

The View from Hong Kong, Mainland China, and Taiwan

Luwei Rose Luqiu

LONDON AND NEW YORK

First published 2025
by Routledge
4 Park Square, Milton Park, Abingdon, Oxon OX14 4RN

and by Routledge
605 Third Avenue, New York, NY 10158

Routledge is an imprint of the Taylor & Francis Group, an informa business

British Library Cataloguing-in-Publication Data
A catalogue record for this book is available from the British Library

Library of Congress Cataloging-in-Publication Data
Names: Lüqiu, Luwei, author.
Title: Reporting sexual violence and #MeToo in Asia : the view from Hong Kong, mainland China, and Taiwan / Luwei Rose Luqiu.
Description: Abingdon, Oxon ; New York, NY : Routledge, 2025. |
Series: Focus on journalism studies | Includes bibliographical references and index.
Subjects: LCSH: Rape in mass media. | MeToo movement in mass media. | MeToo movement—China—Hong Kong. | Rape culture—China—Hong Kong. | MeToo movement—China. | Rape culture—China. | MeToo movement—Taiwan. | Rape culture—Taiwan.
Classification: LCC P96.R35 L87 2025 (print) | LCC P96.R35 (ebook) |
DDC 362.883920951—dc23/eng/20240923
LC record available at https://lccn.loc.gov/2024041865
LC ebook record available at https://lccn.loc.gov/2024041866

ISBN: 978-1-032-75566-3 (hbk)
ISBN: 978-1-032-75568-7 (pbk)
ISBN: 978-1-003-47456-2 (ebk)

DOI: 10.4324/9781003474562

Typeset in Times New Roman
by codeMantra

Contents

1 Reflecting Change

Media's Role in Addressing Sexual Violence in Chinese Societies

In recent years, there has been a surge in public discourse around sexual violence, propelled by global movements such as #MeToo and heightened awareness due to campaigns for gender rights and equality. This rise in consciousness is reflected in Chinese-speaking societies, where news coverage of sexual violence cases has seen a marked increase. How journalists and newsrooms report these cases and how audiences perceive and interpret them provide a mirror that reflects societal norms and attitudes.

A detailed examination of news media coverage on #MeToo cases can offer valuable insights into the potential role of media in combating rape culture in society and instigating social change. Rape culture refers to a pervasive belief system that normalizes and excuses sexual violence, shaping societal discourse around sexual crimes such as rape and sexual assault. In the news media sphere, manifestations of rape culture can be observed in the tone of coverage, choice of words, the framing of stories, and public debate, which can often tilt toward empathy for the accused and blame on the victims.

There is a growing concern that the news media portrayal of sexual violence might deter victims from speaking out, a theory supported by some previous research. Indicators of rape culture in news media coverage, including victim-blaming, implying victim uniformity, and questioning the victim's credibility, can potentially contribute to the prevalence of sexual violence. However, a comprehensive study focusing on the manifestations of rape culture in news media coverage within Chinese language-speaking societies is currently absent. The comparison of the three societies' social media discourse also has an urgency. News media and social media discourse are critical elements of the public sphere, essential for forming cyberactivism (Langman, 2005).

Women in mainland China joined the global #MeToo movement in 2018, spearheaded by university students battling sexual misconduct. The movement, primarily digital, uses the internet and social media to mobilize, give voice to marginalized experiences, and promote awareness and civic engagement. However, Chinese authorities and influential entities utilize these same digital platforms to counteract the effects of #MeToo allegations, often overshadowing the voices of sexual violence victims.

DOI: 10.4324/9781003474562-1

The reduction in online spaces dedicated to combating sexual harassment mirrors the increasing hostility and misogyny in digital environments. Although there is widespread societal condemnation of sexual harassment, practices such as victim-shaming, witch-hunting, trolling, and doxing continue to thrive (Liao & Luqiu, 2022a). Furthermore, despite navigating a landscape marked by strict online censorship and other unique social and political challenges, activists have continually adapted their strategies to address these issues (Zeng, 2019).

Interestingly, the absence of the #MeToo hashtag in these discussions has not hampered the articulation of feminist concepts and critique of patriarchal institutions. However, the state news media also employs diversionary tactics, such as emphasizing the foreign nature of these cases and illustrating the evolving nature of Chinese digital feminism and the challenges of rallying online activism without a specific hashtag (Han & Liu, 2024).

The #MeToo movement gained traction in Hong Kong six months after it became globally recognized. It was championed by notable figures like star hurdler Vera Lui, who shared their experiences of sexual harassment on Facebook using the #MeToo hashtag in late 2017. Initial support for these posts was soon overwhelmed by negative and victim-blaming comments, showcasing a culture of online judgment that discourages victims from sharing their experiences and highlights selective law enforcement by the Hong Kong Police (Tsui, 2020).

Despite this, societal attitudes did not immediately shift. The #MeToo movement has been relatively muted in Hong Kong, but its effects are still palpable. According to the Hong Kong Association Concerning Sexual Violence Against Women, with one in seven women experiencing sexual assault, 90% choose not to report it. Many victims remain silent due to social stigma and victim-shaming, issues exacerbated by the pandemic. Hong Kong activists and social workers are advocating for more government support, including increased funding for NGOs and improved public awareness about sexual harassment and violence.

The #MeToo movement merged with the Anti-Extradition Law protest in 2019, evolving into the #ProtestToo campaign. The movement's development and the collaboration between government, civil society, and media are heavily influenced by sociopolitical circumstances. The failure to address sexual assaults on protestors in 2019 underscores how a shift toward authoritarian governance, like that seen in Beijing, can impede efforts to combat sexual violence (Lai, 2021).

In Taiwan, the #MeToo movement gained momentum in June 2023, triggered by a line from the Netflix show "*Wave Makers*." Despite Taiwan's progressive gender equality laws, sexual harassment is still prevalent, with many victims hesitant to report it due to fear of repercussions and societal norms (Huang, 2021). The movement primarily evolved on social media platforms, enabling victims to share their experiences and challenge mainstream narratives and societal taboos around sex and sexual violence.

Media coverage amplified these voices, triggering public debates and government pressure. Following allegations involving the Democratic Progressive Party (DPP), then President Tsai Ing-wen pledged a zero-tolerance policy on sexual harassment, leading to the amendment of Taiwan's anti-sexual harassment laws in July 2023.

Nevertheless, the journey toward gender and sexual equality in Taiwan is just beginning. The role of media, especially social media, in advancing this conversation has provided survivors a platform to share their experiences. The ongoing discourse on #MeToo in Taiwan underscores the need for societal change and the power of media to facilitate this transformation.

As Chinese-speaking societies, mainland China, Hong Kong, and Taiwan share many cultural characteristics. For example, there is a traditional mentality that men are superior to women, and women who do not get married by a certain age are often discriminated against in society. However, there are many differences between the three places. For example, Hong Kong is more influenced by Western culture, which gives women more opportunities to receive an education, establish their economic status, and rise to the top. In Taiwan, because of the development of civil society, women's rights are protected by law. In mainland China, women are still in a relatively subordinate family role. The news media plays different roles in the three places due to the various media systems. Therefore, it is possible to explore the feasibility of the news media's relation to rape culture by comparing how sex crimes are reported in the three places.

News Reporting on Sexual Violence in Hong Kong, Taiwan, and Mainland China

In mainland China, there has been scholarly concern about how the news media should report sexual assault cases since 2010. For instance, when the *Southern Metropolis Daily* graphically reported that a member of the joint defense team, a civil security force established by the government to assist in maintaining social stability, committed rape in the presence of the woman's husband, scholars noted that public criticism was directed at the victim instead of the perpetrator. They criticized the news media that did not see the social problems reflected in the incident, suggesting that the market-oriented media had abandoned their adherence to journalistic ethics for market interests (Yang, 2018; Yang & Zhuo, 2017). In contrast, an analysis of rape news reports from 2014 to 2017 revealed that most of the rape news reports in the Chinese mainland media showed a stereotypical image of female victims, reflecting a "selective construction" process of news media coverage of news events, indicating that some domestic news media still had a patriarchal attitude in their coverage of such events. Patriarchal characteristics are still present in the media coverage of such events, and patriarchal ideas are also shaped through various syntactic forms. In addition, the phenomenon of openly selling victims' privacy in news reports exists, and the news media use different news narratives to create the image of "imperfect victims" (Ye, 2018).

Despite these studies and findings, they have yet to influence the news media significantly. On the one hand, there is no effective conduit for academic research to provoke industry responses. Stringent government regulation of the media in mainland China precludes the existence of any industry association that could jointly establish ethical standards for news media and journalists. Additionally, research indicates that journalism students in mainland China tend to adopt a more permissive and nonchalant attitude toward controversial news reporting practices than their counterparts in some other countries. The findings imply that the educational and experiential background of these students in mainland China significantly shapes their ethical views on journalism, though often with negative impacts (Wu & Weaver, 1998).

In Hong Kong, studies of news media reporting violence against women are rare. Content analysis of news stories on violence against women between 1981 and 1990 found that the discourse in newspapers tended to view violence against women as a private rather than public issue (Chung, 1997). A recent frame analysis was conducted on a Hong Kong newspaper to determine whether news coverage of female fatalities at the hands of their intimate partners was reported in conventional domestic violence ways or if there were culture-specific explanations. Overall, most coverages supported known views of domestic violence, justifying the perpetrator and categorizing the incidents as isolated crimes, which is consistent with rape culture (Hernández, 2018). There are some studies on rape culture, but they are all from a legal and cultural perspective (Chiu, 2004; Chui et al., 2015; Stockbridge, 1994; Tan, 2020). Unlike mainland China, the Hong Kong government does not censor and regulate the news media directly, but different news media industry associations set rules for the industry. For reports involving sexual violence, the Hong Kong Journalists Association has a code of ethics which includes: "Journalists should not pander to prurience, indecency, and sensationalism when reporting news, especially when it involves violence, sex-related crime or suicide" (HKJA).

There are many studies on how sexual assault is reported in the news media in Taiwan. A comparison of different newspapers reveals that there is indeed an intention to make sexual assault news a selling point to attract readers. Among them, *Apple Daily*, regarded as the representative of commercial media, has the most coverage and is most likely to put it on the front page. It also has multiple sources of information; it has the most coverage of forced sexual intercourse cases and more coverage of sexual assault cases involving the abuse of power and influence. *Apple Daily's* reports strengthen the combination of text and images to produce sensationalized and dramatized sexual assault news. With the rise of victim protection awareness, the study concludes that there are still rape myths that are difficult to deconstruct in Taiwan's media coverage of sexual assault cases (Tsai & Su, 2016). The study analyzed Taiwanese newspaper coverage of sexual harassment, revealing persistent myths and a shift in focus from public places to workplaces following the #MeToo movement, with reduced story detail post-movement (Wang, 2021). The study also found that pressures of journalistic competition, power interactions in the field, journalistic regulations, interactions between news outlets and journalists, learning behaviors in the field, and the influence of personal experiences and newspaper organizations impact the reported rape myths. In addition, almost all journalists covering the general news in Taiwan have no gender or feminism education, making it possible to change the reproduction of others' rape myths solely by freeing the mind, not by consciously achieving gender equality (Chiang, 2009). Unlike in mainland China, where academic research has a channel to enter the public discourse and thus influence the media, civil society organizations in Taiwan have been very active in intervening in how the media reports sexual violence. In 2009, civil society organizations in Taiwan suggested that the media should not use the word "rape" to report on sexual assault cases, indicating that the term "sexual assault" and "sexual violence" should be used instead to avoid causing secondary harm to the victims. The media positively responded to this call (Apple Daily, 2009).

Rape Myths, Sexual Violence, and News Reporting

The concept of rape myths emerged in the 1970s, introduced by sociologists like Schwendinger and Schwendinger (1974) and feminists like Brownmiller (1975). These myths encompass a set of cultural beliefs that support male sexual violence against women. They include notions such as the victim's consent, the idea that women invite rape, and the portrayal of rapists and victims. They theorized that rape myths serve to perpetuate male aggression by blaming the victim, absolving the perpetrator, and justifying the violence. These myths parallel other constructs in the social scientific literature, such as just world beliefs and victim-blaming ideologies (Lerner, 1980; Ryan, 1976).

Rape myths encompass a range of false beliefs and attitudes that contribute to victim-blaming, minimizing the seriousness of sexual assault and justifying or excusing the actions of perpetrators (Burt, 1980). These myths often revolve around victim behavior, consent, and the circumstances surrounding the assault (Payne et al., 1999).

News reporting plays a crucial role in shaping public opinion and understanding of sexual violence (Cuklanz, 1996). Unfortunately, media representations often perpetuate rape myths, reinforcing harmful stereotypes and biases. News coverage frequently emphasizes victim characteristics or behaviors, which can perpetuate the myth that victims are somehow responsible for the assault to form victim-blaming (Dukes & Gaither, 2017; Lumsden & Morgan, 2017; Schwark & Bohner, 2019). Victim-blaming language and narratives not only shift blame away from perpetrators but also contribute to the stigmatization and silencing of survivors (Koss et al., 1988).

The perpetuation of rape myths in media reporting has significant implications for survivors, public attitudes, and policy responses. It can discourage survivors from reporting their experiences due to fear of judgment and disbelief (Lonsway & Fitzgerald, 1994). Moreover, it reinforces harmful societal attitudes that contribute to a culture of silence and impunity surrounding sexual violence. The misrepresentation of sexual assault in the media can also influence public opinion, shape societal norms, and hinder efforts to promote prevention and support services.

Sexual violence is a pervasive issue that predominantly affects women, with men's power and women's resistance being critical factors within the social context (Kelly, 1988). The definition of sexual violence has changed over time in response to growing societal awareness and understanding. Initially, it was primarily understood as acts involving forced penetration or physical coercion. However, contemporary definitions have expanded to encompass a broader range of non-consensual sexual acts and exploitative behaviors.

The World Health Organization (WHO, 2002) provides a widely cited definition of sexual violence as "any sexual act, attempt to obtain a sexual act, or other act directed against a person's sexuality using coercion, by any person regardless of their relationship to the victim, in any setting" (p. 5). This definition emphasizes the importance of consent and recognizes that sexual violence can occur within various relationships and contexts.

UNICEF also offers a comprehensive definition of sexual violence, which includes acts such as rape, unwanted touching of private parts, being forced to have sex, being forced to witness sexual violations, and being coerced into nudity (UNICEF, p. 1). This definition underscores the central role of consent and acknowledges that sexual violence extends beyond physical force to include manipulation, threats, and power differentials.

The #MeToo movement, gaining significant momentum in recent years, has played a crucial role in expanding the understanding of sexual violence. It has shed light on the prevalence of harassment, coercion, and non-physical forms of sexual violence. This expanded perspective recognizes that sexual violence encompasses not only overt acts of physical force but also psychological, emotional, and verbal forms of abuse (Alaggia & Wang, 2020; Gash & Harding, 2018).

The lexical choices in reports of sexual assault cases reflect mutual influences between professional practice in making news and public perception of the news stories. Rape reporting is a naming problem, where it is providing the society and the individuals' words. Different choices reproduce different social realities and experiences (Lumsden & Morgan, 2017).

Studies have shown that news coverage of rape and sexual violence constructs and widely distributes rape myths and stereotypes of actors in sexual assault cases, which normalize rape (Carter et al., 1998; Cuklanz, 2020;

Tranchese, 2019). News media reports have perpetrated different framing norms and biases toward the perpetrator and victim. Such reports construct rape myths and create rape culture in general. The rape myths generate false ideas or beliefs about rape that trivialize rape, suggest a rape did not occur or only occurred in a particular context, blame the victim for rape, or reduce the perpetrators' culpability (O'Hara, 2012; Sacks et al., 2018). In a quantitative analysis, Baum et al. (2018) have developed a coding instrument with four main categories to examine whether rape culture can predict rape. The categories are (1) victim-blaming language, (2) empathy for perpetrators, (3) implied victim consent, and (4) questioning of victims' credibility. The incidence of these in news coverage of rape reveals a rape culture in the media, and the rape culture positively correlates with the increase in documented sexual assault cases. These four main categories of rape culture in the media are informed mainly by local norms that shape the languages used in reporting rape.

Victim-blaming is both a means and the end of rape myths and rape culture constructed through media reports of rape and sexual violence. News media tend to show a distorted view of women that often depicts female rape victims as either "virgins," "fallen angels," or "whores" (Benedict, 1992; Hirsch, 1994). These depictions demand that a rape victim should be "perfectly" innocent and constantly defend her innocence to avoid being condemned as a "whore," who is assumed to "bring on" a rape due to her behavior, dress, sexual past, or profession (Benedict, 1992; Franiuk et al., 2008; Hirsch, 1994; Kahlor & Morrison, 2007; Vetten, 1998; Worthington, 2008). Therefore, news media tend to suggest that women avoid dressing in a certain way, engaging in promiscuity, drinking heavily, and being a prostitute if they want to avoid rape—which shifts the responsibility to prevent rape to women and only women. Otherwise, they are "asking for it." Other than such binary representation, many news reports give little agency to the victim as an actor, describe her passively, and give little space to the victim in a report (Breen et al., 2017; Fernández-Fuertes et al., 2020).

How consent is understood and framed is also crucial in news reporting. Many news reports tend to imply consent when reporting sexual assault cases, primarily related to how the victim is portrayed. As mentioned above, if the victim does not conform to a "perfect," "innocent," and "responsible" image, the victim will be considered a "worthy victim" (Hengehold, 2000) who implies consent to sex and is therefore incapable of being raped (Norton & Grant, 2008). Studies on campus rape also point to the skepticism about what consent "really is" in an environment of alcohol abuse and "hookup culture" (Fernández-Fuertes et al., 2020; Northcutt et al., 2019). In general, the news media construct either a "perfect" victim or evidence of sexual precociousness and previous sexual experience of an "imperfect" victim tends to be used to imply consent and invalidate the rape accusation (Korn & Efrat, 2004). The situation becomes even more complicated when, in a social environment such as mainland China, education about sexual consent is rare, and the news largely avoids the topic.

To show empathy for perpetrators implicitly is also part of rape culture in news media. In an early exploration of media frames in news coverage of sexual harassment from 1989 to 1995, Bing and Lombardo (1997) identified four standard frames in media, which redefined the behavior of the alleged perpetrators as something other than harassment. Such a frame justifies sexual violence as "boys will be boys" and emphasizes the misunderstanding between the alleged perpetrator and the victim. This is a theme in many existing works of literature that provide excuses and justifications for violence against women (Scully & Marolla, 1984). Studies have also demonstrated that news reports de-emphasize the role of the perpetrator by humanizing the perpetrator, creating a linguistic separation between the perpetrator and the rape, and placing blame on outside factors (Bonnes, 2013; Rollè et al., 2020). Typically, news reports cover details of the perpetrator's life that suggest he is a good person. Such a description gives the reader an impression that the rapist is "not the type that would rape" and draws attention away from the rape itself (Franiuk et al., 2008, p. 791).

News Media as Gatekeepers

According to liberal theory, the media's primary democratic role is to serve as a watchdog over the state, exposing abuses of authority. While this watchdog role is crucial, it is argued that a democratic media system should also include a specialized media tier that allows different social groups to debate social identity, group interests, political strategies, and normative understanding (Curran,2011, 2023). Gatekeeping refers to the process by which media organizations, editors, and journalists act as gatekeepers who control the flow of news and information to the public (Shoemaker & Vos, 2009). They decide which stories to cover, how to frame, and which aspects to prioritize or omit. Gatekeepers are crucial in shaping the public's access to information and influencing their understanding of events. News values are the criteria and factors that guide journalists and editors in determining which stories are newsworthy and deserving of coverage (Galtung & Ruge, 1965). These values include factors such as timeliness, proximity, prominence, conflict, and human interest. Journalists make subjective judgments based on these news values when selecting and prioritizing stories, which can shape the news agenda and influence public perceptions of current events.

Gatekeepers can shape the news agenda and influence public opinion by choosing what stories to cover, how to frame them, and the prominence given to different issues. Their decisions can have profound implications for the public's understanding of events and the societal discourse surrounding them. Gatekeepers can introduce biases, emphasize specific perspectives, or neglect essential topics, potentially influencing the public's perception of reality

(Janowitz, 1975). Gatekeeping is closely related to the agenda-setting theory, which posits that media influence public opinion by determining the salience and importance of issues (McCombs & Shaw, 1972). Media organizations can shape the public agenda through gatekeeping processes by selecting and emphasizing specific stories while downplaying or ignoring others. This agenda-setting power can have significant implications for public discourse and policy priorities.

With the advent of digital media, gatekeeping processes have undergone significant changes. Online platforms and social media have democratized access to information, allowing for user-generated content and alternative news sources (Bro & Wallberg, 2017; Garimella et al., 2018). In the context of the #MeToo movement, the internet played a crucial role in amplifying the voices and stories of survivors of sexual harassment and assault. Social media platforms allowed individuals to share their experiences using the #MeToo hashtag, gaining significant traction and spreading public discussion. The viral nature of the movement on social media influenced newsroom agenda-setting, leading to increased coverage and public attention to issues related to sexual violence and gender equality (Manikonda et al., 2018).

News media are the gatekeepers who provide quotations and paraphrases from various societal actors. At the same time, they are players participating in framing the issue under discussion. News media operate within the constraints of accepted journalistic practices in their respective countries. Ferree et al. (2002) proposed measuring success in mass media forums by two criteria: standing and framing. Standing is getting the actor's voice in the new story to provide its interpretation and meaning to the events it involves. A group or person being treated as an actor with a voice usually refers to those directly quoted in the story. However, gaining standing only guarantees positive coverage if one gains preferred news media frames. Here, framing implies a range of positions rather than one, allowing for a degree of contention among those who share a standard frame. In measuring the rape culture that exists in the news media, framing allows for the presence of victim-blaming and empathy for the perpetrator in news stories.

Journalists are the gatekeepers of news and the producers of news. The degree to which journalists focus on a social issue determines which actors stand and how they are framed. A study of male and female journalists in India found that when covering rape cases, many male and female journalists acknowledged the existence of sexist norms that govern rape-related reporting in India. Female journalists have been more active in attempting to change the way rape and sexual assault was historically reported by adopting non-traditional reporting perspectives. However, despite this, many of these journalists failed to acknowledge the effects of patriarchal hegemony, and some female journalists, deeply integrated into the system, reveled in their subordinate positions in a male-dominated environment (Fadnis, 2018). Yazidi women who survived ISIS sexual violence shared a contradictory narrative of media engagement as victimization and resistance, which they describe as bargaining at the intersection of patriarchy while pointing to how news media coverage impacts their safety and that of their families (Foster & Minwalla, 2018).

Even if journalists are aware of rape culture and try to produce balanced and accurate news reporting, they are constrained by sources, conventions, and institutions that all constitute challenges. A study on reporting domestic violence in the United States showed that police sources tended to avoid defining domestic violence as such, but problematic sources are still used. In addition, editors scrutinize journalists more because of potential legal repercussions regarding defamation and adherence to court reporting's strict guidelines (Cullen et al., 2019). The numerical dominance of men in journalism, particularly in decision-making roles, also affects newsroom culture and, sometimes, is not conducive to eliminating rape culture in news reporting. A study of Australia's print media newsrooms found that, even though women had entered the industry in unprecedented numbers, hegemonic masculinity continues to shape newsroom culture, which maintains a male-dominated agenda and less diversity in news selection (North, 2009). Journalists in three Chinese language-speaking societies also face individual and organizational constraints in reporting rape cases.

The #MeToo movement has sparked significant scholarly attention and discourse, with numerous studies examining its impact on societal attitudes, media coverage, and legal frameworks (Clark-Parsons, 2021; Gash & Harding, 2018; Reyes-Menendez et al., 2020; Rho et al., 2018). Researchers have explored the origins and spread of the movement (Fileborn & Loney-Howes, 2019; Moore, 2019), its role in raising awareness about sexual harassment and assault (Gallagher et al., 2019; Gleeson & Turner, 2019), and its implications for social change (Fairbairn, 2020; Rottenberg, 2019). Studies have analyzed the use of social media platforms as catalysts for collective action and the mobilization of survivors (Palomino-Manjón, 2022), highlighting the power dynamics and challenges associated with online activism (Lampinen, 2020; Mendes et al., 2018). The literature on #MeToo contributes to a broader understanding of gender dynamics, power structures, and social movements, providing insights into the complexities of addressing sexual violence and fostering inclusive and egalitarian societies.

The #MeToo movement has been extensively studied in both social media and news media, with researchers conducting empirical studies to understand its impact in these domains (Anderson & Toor, 2018; Baik et al., 2022; Cuklanz, 2020; De Benedictis et al., 2019; Hosterman et al., 2018; Manikonda et al., 2018; Mueller et al., 2021). Studies examining the role of social media in the #MeToo movement have explored how platforms like Twitter and Facebook have facilitated the sharing of personal stories (Mueller et al., 2021), the formation of collective identities (Gerbaudo, 2022), and the mobilization of support (Hosterman et al., 2018; Quan-Haase et al., 2021). These studies have shed light on the power of social media in amplifying marginalized voices, fostering solidarity among survivors, and challenging existing power structures. On the other hand, research focused on news media has investigated the framing and coverage of #MeToo in traditional media outlets (Evans, 2018; Hansson et al., 2020). Such studies have explored how news organizations have portrayed the movement, the narratives they have constructed, and how much they have contributed to public awareness and policy changes. By examining the interplay between #MeToo and social and news media, empirical research has provided valuable insights into the dynamics of this influential movement and its broader societal implications (Peters, 2020; Starkey et al., 2019).

Empirical studies have investigated the claim that there has been a noticeable increase in news coverage of sexual violence cases in Chinese-speaking societies, indicating a heightened societal awareness (Liao & Luqiu, 2022b; Wu, 2021; Zeng, 2020). These studies have employed media content analysis and quantitative methods to evaluate the scope and characteristics of news reporting on sexual violence (Deng & Chen, 2023). They have examined various factors, including the prevalence of the #MeToo movement, shifts in public attitudes toward gender and sexual violence, and changes in media practices and policies (Luqiu & Liao, 2021; Tan & Xu, 2023). The findings of these empirical studies have enhanced our nuanced comprehension of the evolving landscape of news coverage on sexual violence in Chinese-speaking societies, emphasizing the potential influence of social movements and growing societal awareness on media agendas and reporting practices. However, it is essential to note that these studies primarily focus on mainland China, leaving a substantial gap in research regarding Taiwan and Hong Kong.

The Comparative Study in Chinese-Speaking Societies

This book is a comprehensive analysis of the role of news media in propagating and treating the global #MeToo movement. This comparative study uniquely spans Hong Kong, Taiwan, and mainland China—three culturally similar yet legally and politically distinct societies—to elucidate the variations in media systems and the influence these differences bear on the role and impact of media in social movements. It aims to serve as an invaluable resource for journalists, editors, news organizations, and the public. Short term, it equips journalists and editors with a more profound understanding of the complex interplay between rape culture and media, enabling them to report on sexual violence more effectively. Medium-term news organizations stand to benefit from the insights gained, fostering a more aware and sensitive newsroom culture and leading to more informed reporting on issues related to sexual violence. Long term, the study contributes to societal understanding of rape culture, promoting a more gender-sensitive society and reducing the prevalence of sexual violence.

This book aims to illuminate the complexities of news production processes and the influence of cultural contexts on media narratives in these societies, contributing to broader media literacy efforts. It also offers invaluable new insights into the relationship between news media and social movements. It promises to improve journalistic practices, enhance public understanding of rape culture, and contribute to the broader academic literature, making it a crucial read for anyone interested in the intersection of media, gender, and social change.

In conducting the research for this book, I employed qualitative methods to gather a comprehensive view of the current state and impact of newsroom culture on the coverage of sexual violence. Semi-structured interviews were conducted with 26 journalists—11 from Taiwan, 10 from Mainland China, and 5 from Hong Kong—to gain insights into the journalistic practices and challenges they face in their respective regions. Additionally, 25 victims of sexual violence were interviewed through semi-structured interviews, including 20 from mainland China and 5 from Taiwan, who had shared their experiences online, providing a crucial perspective on the public and personal impact of media coverage. To complement these interviews, I conducted a content analysis of news reporting in Hong Kong and a case study to identify prevalent narratives and detect patterns in the portrayal of sexual violence in mainland China. This methodology allowed for a robust analysis of both qualitative and quantitative data, offering a nuanced understanding of how different factors within newsroom culture influence the reporting of sensitive issues and the potential reforms needed to enhance media coverage and support for victims.

The introduction section of Chapter 1 encompasses conceptual and theoretical discussions related to the research topic. It begins by exploring the conceptual understanding of sexual violence, including its various dimensions and manifestations. The implications of rape myths and their influence on societal attitudes toward sexual violence are also examined. It further delves into a literature review of the #MeToo discourse, analyzing its origins, development, and impact on social perceptions and activism. Additionally, the chapter explores the theoretical framework of gatekeeping theory, which serves as a foundational concept for the subsequent analysis. To establish the empirical context, the literature review highlights studies that have explored the association between #MeToo and social media, as well as its interaction with traditional news media. Specific attention is given to empirical studies conducted in Chinese-speaking societies, examining the news coverage of sexual violence cases in these contexts. Moreover, the introduction section delves into the emergence of #MeToo-related media mergers within the three Chinese societies, emphasizing the significance of different media systems and political structures and how these differences impact gatekeepers' decisions regarding news coverage.

In Chapter 2, I explore the role of news media in China during the #MeToo movement, particularly through the lens of high-profile cases like Xianzi versus Zhu Jun. It discusses how media coverage occasionally highlights individual allegations and avoids challenging deeper patriarchal and political structures due to stringent censorship laws. The analysis reveals that this cautious reporting approach allows for some public discourse but needs to be more robust to support a sustained social movement. The chapter highlights how challenges such as censorship, slow journalistic responses, and a lack of gender sensitivity in male-dominated newsrooms affect the effectiveness of the media. By examining these dynamics, the chapter provides essential insights into the complexities of media advocacy under authoritarian constraints and its critical yet limited role in advancing social justice in China.

Chapter 3 uses sexual harassment at university orientation camps as a case study to analyze the collaborative roles of government, civil society, and media in addressing sexual violence before and after the 2019 anti-extradition bill protests in Hong Kong. Initially, there was an effective partnership, with each sector playing a vital role, though media coverage had room for improvement. Post-protests, this collaboration has deteriorated, influenced by a political shift that aligns media more closely with government narratives, neglecting structural issues and diminishing civil advocacy. The chapter discusses the implications of reduced media freedom under the National Security Law for public discourse and policy-making on sexual harassment, offering crucial insights into the interplay between social movements, legal reforms, and media freedom for scholars, policymakers, and activists involved in gender studies and human rights.

Chapter 4 critically evaluates the role of Taiwanese news media in the #MeToo movement, highlighting both achievements and limitations. Despite Taiwan's progressive stance on gender equality, the #MeToo movement was slow to gain momentum, a delay attributed to deficiencies in journalistic practices such as quality reporting, sensitivity to gender issues, and the perpetuation of rape myths. Analysis of interviews with journalists and survivors unveils a media landscape that, while free, lacks rigorous journalistic standards necessary for effective reporting. The chapter notes a positive shift in media focus from public incidents to workplace harassment post-#MeToo, reflecting an incomplete yet ongoing transformation. It emphasizes the need for improved journalistic practices that report, educate, and advocate for societal change and justice, providing insights into how Taiwanese media can better support social movements and gender equality.

Chapter 5 conducts a comparative analysis of the news media's role in addressing sexual violence in mainland China, Hong Kong, and Taiwan, particularly post-2017's rise of the #MeToo movement. Utilizing a gatekeeping theoretical framework, it examines the complex interplay between digital activism and traditional media coverage and how this influences public perception and policy on sexual violence in these regions. The study highlights that while digital platforms have empowered activists, especially in China, severe state censorship and lack of independent media significantly hinder progress. Conversely, Hong Kong and Taiwan offer more dynamic media environments that facilitate broader public discourse and influence on policy. However, recent democratic backsliding in Hong Kong is restricting the news media's effectiveness in promoting social change, including discussions on sexual violence. This chapter emphasizes the critical role of news media in combating sexual violence. It explores the varied external and internal challenges impacting their efficacy, underscoring the need for maintaining high journalistic standards in liberal democracies to ensure the media's effective gatekeeping role.

In the final chapter, I critique newsroom culture's impact on reporting sexual violence, emphasizing the need for improved gender awareness within journalism. It highlights the challenges in mainland China, Hong Kong, and Taiwan, pointing out the dominant perpetrator-centric media narratives. Advocating for victim-centered reporting, it proposes reforms such as democratizing pitch processes, enhancing gender diversity in leadership, and fostering environments supportive of investigative reporting. Additional suggestions include institutional support such as codes of ethics, legal and mental health resources, and mandatory gender studies in journalism education. These measures aim to elevate media coverage quality on gender issues, fostering societal and legislative advancements for a more equitable media landscape.

References

Alaggia, R., & Wang, S. (2020). "I never told anyone until the# metoo movement": What can we learn from sexual abuse and sexual assault disclosures made through social media? *Child Abuse & Neglect*, *103*, 104312.

Anderson, M., & Toor, S. (2018). How social media users have discussed sexual harassment since# MeToo went viral. https://www.pewresearch.org/short-reads/2018/10/11/how-social-media-users-have-discussed-sexual-harassment-since-metoo-went-viral/

Apple Daily. (2009). The naming of the media offensive words "rape," "obscene," and "breast rubbing" is on the list. *Apple Daily*.

Baik, J. M., Nyein, T. H., & Modrek, S. (2022). Social media activism and convergence in tweet topics after the initial# MeToo movement for two distinct groups of Twitter users. *Journal of Interpersonal Violence*, *37*(15–16), NP13603–NP13622.

Baum, M. A., Cohen, D. K., & Zhukov, Y. M. (2018). Rape culture and sexual crime. Retrieved from https://scholar.harvard.edu/files/mbaum/files/rapecultureqjps_appendix.pdf

Benedict, H. (1992). *Virgin or vamp: How the press covers sex crimes*. Oxford University Press.

Bing, J. M., & Lombardo, L. X. (1997). Talking past each other about sexual harassment: An exploration of frames for understanding. *Discourse & Society*, *8*(3), 293–311.

Bonnes, S. (2013). Gender and racial stereotyping in rape coverage: An analysis of rape coverage in a South African newspaper, Grocott's Mail. *Feminist Media Studies*, *13*(2), 208–227.

Breen, M. D., Easteal, P., Holland, K., Sutherland, G., & Vaughan, C. (2017). Exploring Australian journalism discursive practices in reporting rape: The pitiful predator and the silent victim. *Discourse & Communication*, *11*(3), 241–258.

Bro, P., & Wallberg, F. (2017). Digital gatekeeping: News media versus social media. In Bob Franklin. *The future of journalism: In an age of digital media and economic uncertainty* (pp. 337–345). Routledge.

Brownmiller, S. (1975). *Against our will: Men, women, and rape*. Simon & Schuster.

Burt, M. R. (1980). Cultural myths and supports for rape. *Journal of Personality and Social Psychology, 38*(2), 217.

Carter, C., Branston, G., & Allan, S. (1998). Setting new(s) agendas: an introduction. In Carter, C., Branston, G., & Allan, S. (Eds.). *News, gender, and power* (pp. 1–13). New York: Routledge.

Chiang, Y. (2009). *Rape myth of sexual assault news and its influential factors in the news field.* (Master's thesis, National Taiwan University). Retrieved from https://www.airitilibrary.com/Publication/alDetailedMesh1?DocID=U0001-1102200922345200

Chiu, M. C. (2004). Contextualising the rhetoric of sexual violence in Hong Kong. *China: An International Journal, 2*(1), 83–107.

Chui, W. H., Cheng, K. K. Y., & Ong, Y. R. (2015). Attitudes of the Hong Kong Chinese public towards sex offending policies: The role of stereotypical views of sex offenders. *Punishment & Society, 17*(1), 94–113.

Chung, C. Y. (1997). Combating violence against women: Hindsight from a decade of news reports on family violence in Hong Kong. *The Hong Kong Journal of Social Work, 31*(01n02), 83–96.

Clark-Parsons, R. (2021). "I see you, I believe you, I stand with you":# MeToo and the performance of networked feminist visibility. *Feminist Media Studies, 21*(3), 362–380.

Cuklanz, L. (1996). *Rape on trial: How the mass media construct legal reform and social change*. University of Pennsylvania Press.

Cuklanz, L. (2020). Problematic news framing of# MeToo. *The Communication Review, 23*(4), 251–272.

Cullen, P., O'Brien, A., & Corcoran, M. (2019). Reporting on domestic violence in the Irish media: An exploratory study of journalists' perceptions and practices. *Media, Culture & Society, 41*(6), 774–790.

Curran, J. (2011). *Media and democracy*. Taylor & Francis.

Curran, J. (2023). Rethinking media and democracy. In Ralph Negrine, James Stanyer. *The political communication reader* (pp. 27–31). Routledge.

De Benedictis, S., Orgad, S., & Rottenberg, C. (2019). # MeToo, popular feminism and the news: A content analysis of UK newspaper coverage. *European Journal of Cultural Studies, 22*(5–6), 718–738.

Deng, Y., & Chen, R. (2023). Did# METOO advance the feminist movement in China? A typical Chinese case study of sexual harassment. Impact of power relations and morality. *Methaodos. Revista de Ciencias Sociales, 11*(1), 2.

Dukes, K. N., & Gaither, S. E. (2017). Black racial stereotypes and victim blaming: Implications for media coverage and criminal proceedings in cases of police violence against racial and ethnic minorities. *Journal of Social Issues, 73*(4), 789–807.

Evans, A. (2018). # MeToo: A study on sexual assault as reported in the New York Times. *Occam's Razor, 8*(1), 3.

Fadnis, D. (2018). Uncovering rape culture: Patriarchal values guide Indian media's rape-related reporting. *Journalism Studies, 19*(12), 1750–1766.

Fairbairn, J. (2020). Before# MeToo: Violence against women social media work, bystander intervention, and social change. *Societies, 10*(3), 51.

Fernández-Fuertes, A. A., Fernández-Rouco, N., Lázaro-Visa, S., & Gómez-Pérez, E. (2020). Myths about sexual aggression, sexual assertiveness, and sexual violence in adolescent romantic relationships. *International Journal of Environmental Research and Public Health*, *17*(23), 8744.

Ferree, M. M., Gamson, W. A., Rucht, D., & Gerhards, J. (2002). *Shaping abortion discourse: Democracy and the public sphere in Germany and the United States*. Cambridge University Press.

Fileborn, B., & Loney-Howes, R. (2019). Introduction: Mapping the emergence of# MeToo. In Bianca Fileborn, Rachel Loney-Howes. *#MeToo and the politics of social change* (pp. 1–18). Palgrave Macmillan, London.

Foster, J. E., & Minwalla, S. (2018, March). Voices of Yazidi women: Perceptions of journalistic practices in the reporting on ISIS sexual violence. *Women's Studies International Forum*, *67*, 53–64. Pergamon.

Franiuk, R., Seefelt, J. L., Cepress, S. L., & Vandello, J. A. (2008). Prevalence and effects of rape myths in print journalism: The Kobe Bryant case. *Violence against Women*, *14*(3), 287–309.

Gallagher, R. J., Stowell, E., Parker, A. G., & Foucault Welles, B. (2019). Reclaiming stigmatized narratives: The networked disclosure landscape of# MeToo. *Proceedings of the ACM on Human-Computer Interaction*, *3*(CSCW), 1–30.

Galtung, J., & Ruge, M. H. (1965). The structure of foreign news: The presentation of the Congo, Cuba and Cyprus crises in four Norwegian newspapers. *Journal of Peace Research*, *2*(1), 64–90.

Garimella, K., De Francisci Morales, G., Gionis, A., & Mathioudakis, M. (2018, April). Political discourse on social media: Echo chambers, gatekeepers, and the price of bipartisanship. In *Proceedings of the 2018 world wide web conference* (pp. 913–922).

Gash, A., & Harding, R. (2018). # MeToo? Legal discourse and everyday responses to sexual violence. *Laws*, *7*(2), 21.

Gerbaudo, P. (2022). From individual affectedness to collective identity: Personal testimony campaigns on social media and the logic of collection. *New Media & Society*, *26*(8), 4904–4921. https://doi.org/10.1177/14614448221128523.

Gleeson, J., & Turner, B. (2019). Online feminist activism as performative consciousness-raising: A# MeToo case study. In Bianca Fileborn, Rachel Loney-Howes *#MeToo and the politics of social change* (pp. 53–69). Palgrave Macmillan, London

Han, L., & Liu, Y. (2024). # metoo activism without the# MeToo hashtag: online debates over entertainment celebrities' sex scandals in China. *Feminist Media Studies*, 24(4), 657–674.

Hansson, K., Sveningsson, M., Ganetz, H., & Sandgren, M. (2020). Legitimising a feminist agenda: The# metoo petitions in Sweden 2017–2018. *Nordic Journal of Media Studies*, *2*(1), 121–132.

Hengehold, L. (2000). Remapping the event: Institutional discourses and the trauma of rape. *Signs: Journal of Women in Culture and Society*, *26*(1), 189–214.

Hernández, M. (2018). "Killed out of love": A frame analysis of domestic violence coverage in Hong Kong. *Violence against Women*, *24*(12), 1454–1473.

Hirsch, S. F. (1994). Interpreting media representations of a "night of madness": Law and culture in the construction of rape identities. *Law & Social Inquiry*, *19*(4), 1023–1056.

HKJA. Joint code of ethics of the four journalistic originations. Retrieved from https://www.hkja.org.hk/en/code-of-ethics/joint-code-of-ethics-of-the-4-journalistic-organizations/

Hosterman, A. R., Johnson, N. R., Stouffer, R., & Herring, S. (2018). Twitter, social support messages, and the# MeToo movement. *The Journal of Social Media in Society*, *7*(2), 69–91.

Huang, C. L. (2021). # MeToo in East Asia: The politics of speaking out. *Politics & Gender*, *17*(3), 483–490.

Janowitz, M. (1975). Professional models in journalism: The gatekeeper and the advocate. *Journalism Quarterly*, *52*(4), 618–626.

Kahlor, L., & Morrison, D. (2007). Television viewing and rape myth acceptance among college women. *Sex Roles*, *56*(11), 729–739.

Kelly, L. (2013). *Surviving sexual violence*. John Wiley & Sons.

Korn, A., & Efrat, S. (2004). The coverage of rape in the Israeli popular press. *Violence Against Women*, *10*(9), 1056–1074.

Koss, M. P., Dinero, T. E., Seibel, C. A., & Cox, S. L. (1988). Stranger and acquaintance rape: Are there differences in the victim's experience? *Psychology of Women Quarterly*, *12*(1), 1–24.

Lai, R. Y. (2021). From# MeToo to# ProtestToo: How a Feminist Movement converged with a pro-democracy protest in Hong Kong. *Politics & Gender*, *17*(3), 500–507.

Lampinen, A. (2020). *Tweeting for change: How Twitter users practice hashtag activism through# BlackLivesMatter and# MeToo* (Master's thesis, A. Lampinen).

Langman, L. (2005). From virtual public spheres to global justice: A critical theory of internetworked social movements. *Sociological Theory*, *23*(1), 42–74.

Lerner, M. J. (1980). *The belief in a just world: A fundamental delusion*. Putnam.

Liao, S., & Luqiu, L. R. (2022a). Four years after #Metoo in China: Shrinking digital space for change. *The Diplomat*. Retrieved from https://thediplomat.com/2022/09/four-years-after-metoo-in-china-shrinking-digital-space-for-change/

Liao, S., & Luqiu, L. R. (2022b). # MeToo in China: The dynamic of digital activism against sexual assault and harassment in higher education. *Signs: Journal of Women in Culture and Society*, *47*(3), 741–764.

Lonsway, K. A., & Fitzgerald, L. F. (1994). Rape myths. In review. *Psychology of Women Quarterly*, *18*(2), 133–164.

Lumsden, K., & Morgan, H. (2017). Media framing of trolling and online abuse: Silencing strategies, symbolic violence, and victim blaming. *Feminist Media Studies*, *17*(6), 926–940.

Luqiu, L. R., & Liao, S. X. (2021). Rethinking 'the personal is political:' Enacting agency in the narrative of sexual harassment experiences in China. *Discourse & Society*, *32*(6), 708–727.

Manikonda, L., Beigi, G., Liu, H., & Kambhampati, S. (2018). Twitter for sparking a movement, reddit for sharing the moment: # metoo through the lens of social media. *arXiv preprint arXiv:1803.08022*.

McCombs, M. E., & Shaw, D. L. (1972). The agenda-setting function of mass media. *Public Opinion Quarterly*, *36*(2), 176–187.

Mendes, K., Ringrose, J., & Keller, J. (2018). # MeToo and the promise and pitfalls of challenging rape culture through digital feminist activism. *European Journal of Women's Studies*, *25*(2), 236–246.

Moore, J. D. (2019). # MeToo, but was I included? The rhetorical framing of the origins of the Me Too movement.

Mueller, A., Wood-Doughty, Z., Amir, S., Dredze, M., & Nobles, A. L. (2021). Demographic representation and collective storytelling in the me too Twitter hashtag activism movement. *Proceedings of the ACM on Human-Computer Interaction*, *5*(CSCW1), 1–28.

North, L. (2009). 'Blokey' newsroom culture. *Media International Australia, 132*(1), 5–15.

Northcutt Bohmert, M., Allison, K., & Ducate, C. (2019). "A rape was reported": Construction of crime in a university newspaper. *Feminist Media Studies, 19*(6), 873–889.

Norton, R., & Grant, T. (2008). Rape myth in true and false rape allegations. *Psychology, Crime & Law, 14*(4), 275–285.

O'Hara, S. (2012). Monsters, playboys, virgins, and whores: Rape myths in the news media's coverage of sexual violence. *Language and Literature, 21*(3), 247–259.

Palomino-Manjón, P. (2022). Feminist activism on Twitter: The discursive construction of sexual violence and victim-survivors in# WhyIDidntReport. *Journal of Language Aggression and Conflict, 10*(1), 140–168.

Payne, D. L., Lonsway, K. A., & Fitzgerald, L. F. (1999). Rape myth acceptance: Exploration of its structure and its measurement using the Illinois rape myth acceptance scale. *Journal of Research in Personality, 33*(1), 27–68.

Peters, M. V. (2020). From the whisper network to# MeToo: Framing gender, gossip, and sexual harassment. *European Journal of American Studies*, https://journals.openedition.org/ejas/16587

Quan-Haase, A., Mendes, K., Ho, D., Lake, O., Nau, C., & Pieber, D. (2021). Mapping# MeToo: A synthesis review of digital feminist research across social media platforms. *New Media & Society, 23*(6), 1700–1720.

Reyes-Menendez, A., Saura, J. R., & Thomas, S. B. (2020). Exploring key indicators of social identity in the# MeToo era: Using discourse analysis in UGC. *International Journal of Information Management, 54*, 102129.

Rho, E. H. R., Mark, G., & Mazmanian, M. (2018). Fostering civil discourse online: Linguistic behavior in comments of# metoo articles across political perspectives. *Proceedings of the ACM on Human-Computer Interaction, 2*(CSCW), 1–28.

Rollè, L., Santoniccolo, F., D'Amico, D., & Trombetta, T. (2020). News media representation of domestic violence victims and perpetrators: Focus on gender and sexual orientation in international literature. In Nicole Moulding. *Gendered Domestic Violence and Abuse in Popular Culture* (pp. 149–169). Routledge, UK.

Rottenberg, C. (2019). # MeToo and the prospects of political change. *Soundings, 71*(71), 40–49.

Ryan, W. (1976). *Blaming the victim*. Random House.

Sacks, M., Ackerman, A. R., & Shlosberg, A. (2018). Rape myths in the media: A content analysis of local newspaper reporting in the United States. *Deviant Behavior, 39*(9), 1237–1246.

Schwark, S., & Bohner, G. (2019). Sexual violence—"victim" or "survivor": News images affect explicit and implicit judgments of blame. *Violence against Women, 25*(12), 1491–1509.

Schwendinger, J. R., & Schwendinger, H. (1974). Rape myths: In legal, theoretical, and everyday practice. *Crime and Social Justice, 1*, 18–26.

Scully, D., & Marolla, J. (1984). Convicted rapists' vocabulary of motive: Excuses and justifications. *Social Problems, 31*(5), 530–544.

Shoemaker, P. J., & Vos, T. (2009). *Gatekeeping theory*. Routledge.

Starkey, J. C., Koerber, A., Sternadori, M., & Pitchford, B. (2019). # MeToo goes global: Media framing of silence breakers in four national settings. *Journal of Communication Inquiry, 43*(4), 437–461.

Stockbridge, S. (1994). Rape and representation: The regulation of Hong Kong films in Hong Kong and Australia. *Asian Studies Review*, *17*(3), 43–49.

Tan, N. N. H. (2020). *Resisting rape culture: The Hebrew Bible and Hong Kong sex workers*. Routledge.

Tan, Y., & Xu, K. (2023). # Metoo as communities of practice: A study of Chinese victims' digital narratives of sexual harassment. *Journal of Applied Communication Research*, *51*(3), 302–319.

Tranchese, A. (2019). Covering rape: How the media determine how we understand sexualised violence. *Gender and Language*, *13*(2), 174–201.

Tsai, Y. W., & Su, H. (2016). Evolution of rape myths and sexual assaults in newspaper coverage. *Mass Communication Research*, *2016*(128), 85–134.

Tsui, C. Y. (2020). Judging the online judges: The two #metoo cases in Hong Kong. *FACTA University-Philosophy, Sociology, Psychology and History*, *19*(3), 241–255.

UNICEF. 12 questions and answers about sexual violence. Retrieved from https://www.unicef.org/eca/media/10251/file/QA%20Sexual%20Violence%20EN.pdf

Vetten, L. (1998). The rape surveillance project. *Agenda*, *13*(36), 45–49.

Wang, S. Y. (2021). Content and trend analysis of newspaper coverage of sexual harassment incidents in Taiwan. *Taiwan Journal of Sexology*, *27*(1), 23–49. https://doi.org/10.3966/160857872021052701002

WHO. (2002). World report on violence and health. *World Health Organization.* Retrieved from https://iris.who.int/bitstream/handle/10665/42495/9241545615_eng.pdf?sequence=1

Worthington, N. (2008). Encoding and decoding rape news: How progressive reporting inverts textual orientations. *Women's Studies in Communication*, *31*(3), 344–367.

Wu, W. (2021). *Framing# MeToo Movement in China: A content analysis of China women's news coverage* (Doctoral dissertation, University of South Florida).

Wu, W., & Weaver, D. H. (1998). Making Chinese journalists for the next millennium: The professionalization of Chinese journalism students. *Gazette (Leiden, Netherlands)*, *60*(6), 513–529.

Yang, M. M. (2018). A study of mainstream media coverage of Child sexual abuse issues in China. (Master's thesis. Chongqing University). Retrieved from https://cdmd.cnki.com.cn/Article/CDMD-10611-1018854503.htm

Yang, M. M., & Zhuo, G. J. (2017). A study of social memory of sexually abused children in the media perspective. *Contemporary Youth Studies*. Retrieved from https://is.sass.org.cn/2017/0830/c3122a81058/page.htm

Ye, B. B. (2018). A Framing analysis of sexual assault coverage in *Southern Metropolitan Daily.* (Master's thesis. Xinjiang University of Finance and Economics). Retrieved from https://xueshu.baidu.com/usercenter/paper/show?paperid=1e7j0t70y5390vv0wu5s0ac06b081230&site=xueshu_se

Zeng, J. (2019). You say# MeToo, I say# MiTu: China's online campaigns against sexual abuse. In Bianca Fileborn, Rachel Loney-Howes. *# MeToo and the politics of social change* (pp. 71–83). Palgrave Macmillan, London.

Zeng, J. (2020). Bianca Fileborn, Rachel Loney-Howes # MeToo as connective action: A study of the anti-sexual violence and anti-sexual harassment campaign on Chinese social media in 2018. *Journalism Practice*, *14*(2), 171–190. Palgrave Macmillan, London

2 Mainland China

Does News Media Still Have the Potential to Facilitate Change?

On a June afternoon in 2024, six girls were sitting in a Starbucks in a commercial building on the outskirts of Beijing. They had just arrived from the nearby Beijing Court. At that time, a defamation lawsuit was underway inside the court. The plaintiff was Li Songwei, a renowned psychologist, and the defendant was his former client Wang Xinmiao, known online as "Dongni." In July 2022, Dongni accused Li Songwei on the internet of having an intimate relationship with her during their consultation sessions. This accusation was denied, and in September 2023, she was sued by Li Songwei (The Paper, 2024).

These six girls were supporters of Dongni, previously strangers to each other; five of them had not known Dongni before. From the first court hearing, they moved from online to offline supporters. Since the court hearings were closed to the public, they could only stand at the entrance to cheer for Dongni as she entered the court. They discussed the case with three young reporters inside the cafe while three Japanese reporters in Beijing sat nearby. I was invited to join and hoped to share with the reporters how to cover issues of sexual violence. Although these supporters also spoke out for Dongni through social media, seeking public support and gaining attention from the news media were even more crucial. However, finding the appropriate news angle while balancing the reportage posed significant challenges for the reporters.

The supporters and reporters view this case as continuing China's #MeToo movement. After a brief surge of #MeToo news coverage in 2018, #MeToo has become a sensitive term in China. However, this does not prevent the exposure of individual #MeToo cases that have attracted global attention but are less known in China, such as the sexual assault allegations made by tennis player Peng Shuai against former Vice Premier Zhang Gaoli. This globally covered case is off-limits for Chinese media, highlighting the selective censorship often imposed on high-profile political figures (Davidson, 2021). However, cases like Dongni's accusations against Li Songwei can be circulated online and reported by the news media because Li Songwei does not belong to the system; he is a private practitioner and a well-known public figure.

DOI: 10.4324/9781003474562-2

Among these six girls, one is known online as "Xianzi," whose real name is Zhou Xiaoxuan. Xianzi had a similar experience to Dongni. In July 2018, when the #MeToo movement reached China, Xianzi accused Zhu Jun, a host at the state media, *Chinese Central Television (CCTV)*, of indecent behavior toward her during her internship at *CCTV* in 2014 through Sina Weibo. As a result, she was sued by Zhu Jun, and her case against Zhu Jun was called a landmark sexual harassment allegation in China by international media. In this chapter, I use the Xianzi case as a case study to show the role of news media in mainland China during the #MeToo movement.

News Media as the Potential Facilitator of Social Change

In the context of the #MeToo movement in China, the role of news media has been multifaceted and complex, shaped by the country's stringent censorship laws and the government's tight grip on public discourse (Wu, 2021). This section explores the dual role of news media during the #MeToo movement in China: as a controlled entity under the authoritarian regime and as a potential facilitator of social change, albeit within certain constraints (Liao & Luqiu, 2022).

The Chinese news media, predominantly state-owned or state-affiliated, operates under strict regulatory frameworks that dictate the boundaries of permissible content. These media outlets acted as cautious observers during the #MeToo movement. News organizations treated the explosive allegations surfacing on social media platforms like Weibo lightly, reflecting the state's ambivalence toward the burgeoning movement (Chen & Wang, 2020).

The government's control over the news media is pivotal in understanding its initial silence and subsequent selective reporting on #MeToo cases. The Chinese Communist Party (CCP) utilizes media to uphold social stability and reinforce government policies (Caple, 2019). Therefore, when cases like that of Dr. Luo Xixi against Chen Xiaowu at Beihang University emerged in 2018 as the first #MeToo case in China, the news media's coverage was measured, highlighting the government's responsiveness rather than the systemic issues raised by the movement (Liao & Luqiu, 2022).

This control is also evident in the periodic bans and censorship of the #MeToo hashtag and related discussions, which the government justifies as measures to maintain social harmony (Han & Liu, 2024). News outlets, therefore, have to navigate a complex landscape where they balance public interest journalism with the overarching need to comply with censorship laws.

Despite these restrictions, the news media has played a critical role in shaping public awareness and discourse concerning sexual misconduct in higher education and beyond. Liao and Luqiu (2022) studied four sexual harassment cases in Chinese universities before and after the #MeToo movement. They found out that when the news media did cover #MeToo stories, they often focused on individual cases without challenging the broader patriarchal and political structures. This approach aligns with the state's strategy to isolate incidents as anomalies rather than symptoms of widespread societal issues, thus avoiding a direct challenge to the political status quo. However, reporting on these cases, even in a controlled manner, brought visibility to the issues that could not be entirely silenced. The coverage of Dr. Luo's story, for example, while limited, was instrumental in sparking a national conversation about sexual harassment. It demonstrated the potential of news media to bridge isolated digital activism and broader public engagement.

The news media's potential in China to advocate for social change within the context of #MeToo lies in its ability to subtly push the boundaries of discussion. For instance, while direct criticism of the government's handling of sexual harassment cases is off-limits, media outlets can focus on the legal and social reforms needed to protect women, indirectly supporting the movement's goals (Zeng, 2020). Moreover, news media can play a crucial role in educating the public about the nuances of sexual harassment and the legal protections available to victims. By doing so, they can foster a more informed citizenry capable of advocating for change within China's legal frameworks (Ling & Liao, 2020).

The interaction between digital activism and traditional news media offers a glimpse into a potential collaborative synergy. Digital platforms often serve as the initial outlets for victims' stories, which are picked up by news media, lending them greater legitimacy and a wider audience. Although limited by censorship, this synergy is crucial in amplifying survivors' voices and pushing issues onto the national agenda. The major challenge facing news media in China in the context of movements like #MeToo is the state's censorship apparatus (Yin & Sun, 2021). The unpredictability of censorship and the risk of shutdowns or penalties create an environment of self-censorship among journalists. Additionally, the alignment of media with state narratives often leads to underreporting or misreporting of critical issues, thereby diluting the impact of digital activism (Lee et al., 2023).

The role of news media in China during the #MeToo movement symbolizes the broader challenges and potentials inherent in practicing journalism within an authoritarian context. While fundamentally constrained, the news media still holds a critical albeit limited potential to influence public discourse and policy on sexual harassment. Moving forward, the effectiveness of news media as a tool for social change will largely depend on the evolving dynamics between state control and the growing public demand for transparency and justice in cases of sexual misconduct. In this delicate balance, the Chinese news media finds itself at a crossroads, navigating between state directives and the imperative to respond to societal shifts.

In July 2024, Wang Di, a female Ph.D. student at Renmin University, posted a video on social media where she held up her ID card and publicly accused her Ph.D. advisor, Wang Guiyuan, of demanding sexual relations with her. The university responded swiftly to the video, which quickly went viral, announcing that their investigation confirmed the allegations the following day, leading to the faculty member's dismissal. However, neither official reports nor the news media used the term "sexual harassment," merely citing the teacher's "moral flaws." The coverage included only official responses and omitted details of the incident and any mention of the victim (May & Wang, 2024). This case highlights that the #MeToo movement, which began in universities in 2018 as collective action, has not evolved into a sustained social movement capable of establishing mechanisms to handle sexual harassment in higher education and protect victims' rights, primarily those of students. Tightening control over the news media has reduced its role as a facilitator, making social media the primary platform for individuals, including victims of sexual violence, to seek justice.

Xianzi vs. Zhujun: The Symbolic Case of #Metoo in China

The case of Xianzi, like other cases that have emerged in Chinese universities, began with an internet exposé, which then captured the attention of the news media and the public. However, what sets this case apart from others in Chinese higher education is that it proceeded through the judicial system, leading international news media to describe it as a landmark #MeToo case, called Xianzi the #Metoo icon (BBC,2021). This is significant because, rather than relying on institutional and organizational disciplinary systems, like universities firing faculty members due to their "moral flaws" after the exposure of sexual harassment cases, the case was pursued through legal means, aligning with the ultimate goal of the #MeToo movement in China: enabling victims to seek justice through the judiciary. The progress of this case also illustrates how Chinese news media drive social awareness, interact with social media, and are influenced by censorship regulations.

On July 26, 2018, at 6:42 a.m., Xu Chao, a journalist for *Caixin* Magazine and known online as "Mai Shao Tongxue," posted a detailed article on Sina Weibo. The article, which Xu claimed was on behalf of a friend of a friend, exposed *CCTV* host Zhu Jun for sexual harassment. Xu tagged the post with #MeToo and mentioned Zhu Jun's Weibo account. The post did not include the name of its author.

Xuanzi shared the original article on her WeChat Moments. She recounted her experience as an intern in 2014 for *CCTV*'s "Art Life" program, describing an incident of sexual misconduct by Zhu Jun in the *CCTV* makeup room, which only ceased when someone else entered the room. The following day, she reported the incident to the police, who refused to file a case and advised her to drop the matter, citing Zhu Jun's influential position. Zhu Jun, one of China's most renowned TV hosts, has hosted several *CCTV* New Year's Galas, a globally broadcast annual event that selects its hosts through a rigorous process. As such, Zhu Jun became one of the most high-profile figures implicated in China's #MeToo movement, with ties to official circles. As a national television employee, he also held a government office rank.

Unlike *WeChat* Moments, a private messaging platform, *Weibo* is a public social media platform akin to Twitter, now X. The post quickly went viral, attracting thousands of comments within an hour. However, by 8:50 a.m., *Weibo* began deleting the post and removed the topic from trending searches. Xu Chao's original post was made visible only to her. Despite this, the article began circulating widely on the Chinese internet, with Weibo users sharing it. *The Global Times*, under *People's Daily*, published an online article about the allegations against Zhu Jun, quoting netizens and including excerpts from the article. This report was shared by other portal sites, which, lacking official news reporting licenses, could only republish reports from news media all under government control. At 10:46 p.m. that same day, a classmate of Xuanzi also posted a lengthy article on *Weibo* detailing their experiences and the pressure from teachers to remain silent, which was quickly censored.

The following day, *Caixin*, a prominent business magazine, interviewed Xuanzi, which corroborated her story and included interviews with teachers, classmates, and lawyers she had contacted after the incident. The following day, she reported the incident to the police with a lawyer, but the case was dismissed. The report also stated that the journalists had contacted the police but had not received a response (Zhang et al., 2018). *Caixin* also published this report in English (Yuan et al., 2018).

This *Caixin* report stood out because it provided a comprehensive, fact-based account, unlike other media that faced bans. However, five hours after its online publication, the report was deleted. However, the English reporting is still accessible.

A lengthy legal battle ensued. On August 15, Zhu Jun sued Xu Chao and Xuanzi for defamation. On September 25, they received the indictment. Zhu Jun, claiming severe damage to his reputation and emotional distress, filed a civil lawsuit at the Haidian District Court in Beijing, demanding the deletion of related *Weibo* posts, compensation exceeding 650,000 yuan for reputational and emotional damages, and a public apology in newspapers and online. Concurrently, Xuanzi counter-sued Zhu Jun for sexual harassment and infringement of her rights, becoming the first in China to take an alleged harasser to court as a victim.

The case drew significant media attention, both domestic and international, and was accepted by the court on October 25. On December 2, 2020, the first hearing took place, attended by numerous media and supporters of Xuanzi, with over 100 waiting outside the courtroom at peak times. Some of the supporters even hold posters to show their support. The gathering was largely peaceful, though there were scuffles as police tried to clear the protesters and dragged away foreign reporters (Zhao, 2020). However, this spontaneous offline collective action caused concern among the authorities, who worried about the case's power and might cause social instability. Although some Chinese news media reported the trial and the gathering outside the courtroom, the case was not allowed to be reported by Chinese news media after that day. Many accounts that publicly supported Xuanzi were blocked or deleted on Chinese social media. On September 14, 2021, the court ruled that there was insufficient evidence in the first instance and dismissed the case. Xuanzi appealed, and on August 10, 2022, the court held a closed-door second hearing, maintaining the original verdict due to insufficient evidence (Ou, 2021).

News Media as the Facilitator for Public Attention and Government Response

Like university #MeToo cases, internet exposure is just the first step to raising public awareness, necessitating the involvement of credible news media. Hearing one side of the story can evoke empathy and skepticism for the public. Victims' accusations, lacking cross-reference and fact-checking, lead some to doubt their accuracy and fairness. This is particularly common when public figures are involved, whose supporters tend to believe the accused rather than the accuser. When credible news outlets like *Caixin* get involved, providing well-sourced stories—for instance, interviewing classmates whom Xianzi confided in immediately after the incident and teachers who supply additional information—the narrative gains strength. Such details as Xianzi's *WeChat* posts on the day of the incident, which expressed her frustration, prompted her teacher to encourage her to report the incident to the police with a lawyer's help.

In comparison with other cases, Xianzi's had significant backing. Although it occurred four years ago, she had ample witnesses to support her when she approached the police, who initially refused to respond. *Caixin*'s report was retweeted over 11,000 times on *Weibo*. Although it was deleted after five hours, it had already reached a broad audience. The nature of the internet makes it difficult for censors to erase the digital footprint. This detailed report from a reputable media source bolstered support for Xianzi, the victim. The censorship inadvertently caused a backlash, inclining the public more toward Xianzi, sensing that higher-ups were attempting to protect Zhu Jun, and highlighting the unbalanced power dynamics. Xianzi was up against the state machinery.

Despite efforts by censors to quell public discourse, the media worked hard to ensure the voices of Xianzi and Xu Chao were heard. Each act of suppression, threat, or attack against these two women became an opportunity for the media to step in and provide them with a platform to speak out. For example, on August 14, Xu Chao was informed by her landlord that she had to delete posts related to Zhu Jun or face eviction. The next day, *Beijing News*'s *WeChat* public account published an interview with Xu Chao titled "After Zhu Jun Speaks Out, Whistleblower and Parties Involved Seek Legal

Recourse | Exclusive." Although quickly deleted, with persistent arguments from Xu Chao and support from netizens, the landlord withdrew the demand. Later, Xu Chao told another media outlet that the landlord had been informed by a "friend" from the Public Security Bureau and did not want to make trouble to secure the job (Chang, 2021).

On August 15, Zhu Jun's legal team sued Xu Chao and Xianzi, labeling them as the second and third defendants in a case filed at the Beijing Haidian District People's Court. On August 16, Xu Chao posted on *Weibo*, calling for more victims of Zhu Jun's sexual harassment to come forward and contact her and Xianzi. That same day, Xianzi opened a *Weibo* account under "Xianzi and Her Friends" to respond to Zhu Jun's lawyer's statement. That evening, "*Vista Global Politics and Business Think Tank*" released an interview titled "Exclusive Interview with Zhu Jun Sexual Harassment Whistleblower: Will Not Back Down If Brought to Court," which has not been deleted to this day (Bai & Wang, 2021).

This highlights a strategy among Chinese journalists. When mainstream media is tightly controlled, other outlets, not typically focused on politics or serious news, exploit relatively unblocked spaces to keep speaking out. This was similar during the early days of the COVID outbreak, with detailed reporting coming from several magazines less regulated than newspapers and TV stations. With the rise of multimedia, many news outlets began operating their social media accounts, using slightly more lenient online management to publish and spread reports that traditional media could not. Although these posts are often deleted when they become too widespread, it is a race against censorship that has shifted from traditional to social media platforms. Additionally, the prevalence of independent media allows these reports to be shared more widely, as most accounts have few followers, making it still possible to find these reports online.

The Limitations of Social Media in Replacing News Media in China's #MeToo Movement

The case of Xianzi underscores the significant limitations of social media in effectively substituting traditional news media within China's stringent media controls. Despite her and her supporter Xu Chao's efforts to voice concerns on social platforms, the environment needed the balanced and investigative quality that traditional news media typically provides.

Without the impartiality that news media brings as an independent third party, information on social media regarding Xianzi's case was starkly divided between her supporters and those of the accused, Zhu Jun. Each faction presented its narrative, leading to a milieu where personal biases overshadowed factual clarity. The absence of news media's verification processes made it challenging for the public to discern truth purely from facts, often resulting in emotionally or personally biased decisions and opinions.

Social media mainly served to amplify individual voices and forge communities of either support or opposition. However, it failed to facilitate informed discussions or debates about developing workplace anti-harassment policies. Most conversations degenerated into polarized arguments, with each side clinging to their version of events without engaging in constructive dialogue. The lack of news media involvement meant no thorough coverage of judicial proceedings nor insights into their fairness. Crucially, expert analysis that could have shed light on the case's progression and implications needed to be included.

While international media did report on Xianzi's case, offering detailed coverage and identifying it as a pivotal event in China's #MeToo movement, these reports were primarily inaccessible within China due to censorship. This significantly diminished their influence, reducing them to mere documentation rather than a catalyst for change, which might have been possible with extensive local media coverage.

Social media, a decentralized information hub, needs more authoritative influence to sway state policies. News media must elevate online activism into broader public discourse, serving as a forum for effective policy engagement and public education. In China, news media should ideally function like NGOs in democratic societies, empowering and sustaining grassroots digital activism. However, given that news outlets are part of the state apparatus, their power and effectiveness are tied to state interests, complicating their ability to act independently and advocate for social change (Liao & Luqiu, 2022).

Different individuals within state institutions advocating for issues pressure policy-makers to acknowledge their severity, potentially leading to tangible outcomes. While political system outsiders, such as social media influencers and netizens, can initiate digital activism, they need more insider leverage to challenge the status quo. They face increased risks of repression and censorship, especially when perceived as aligned with "overseas forces." Conversely, members within the political system with state benefits, such as news media and university faculty members, can form effective alliances with out-system advocates to pressure other state bodies and switch allegiances if their benefits diminish.

At the brink of authoritarian control, the belief in a fair and just society persists despite the constraints imposed by authorities and the media's silence. For digital activism to succeed and drive positive change in China, it must consider how power dynamics among various stakeholders—like universities, media, policy-makers, and advocates—are balanced and navigated. Moreover, starting from local experiences and working through local cultural contexts are crucial. The #MeToo movement in China, lacking a clear political or policy agenda, often sees its online activism to build transnational ties falter, undermining the momentum gained from earlier movements.

In Xianzi's case, although social media provided some visibility and support, it could not replace news media's critical role in offering a balanced, fact-checked, and comprehensive platform for public discourse and systemic change. The lack of robust media coverage within China severely limited the potential for social media to drive the #MeToo movement forward, underscoring the urgent need for free and independent journalism to foster societal progress and accountability.

The Role of Journalists: Activists or Reporters?

Xianzi's case gained significant public attention through Xu Chao, a journalist and prominent *Weibo* blogger. Her role as a journalist contributed to her extensive social media following. The day after she highlighted Xianzi's ordeal, her employer, *Caixin*, released a comprehensive news report. Xu Chao did not participate in this report to avoid a conflict of interest. Nevertheless, her dual role as a whistleblower and journalist conflicted with her professional duties. This situation prompts a critical question: Should journalists use their personal social media accounts to share a victim's narrative unilaterally? Following a defamation lawsuit by Zhu Jun, *Caixin* chose not to use the published reports and interviews as defense evidence, viewing Xu Chao's actions as separate from her professional responsibilities. Subsequently, Xu Chao left *Caixin* to pursue studies in France.

Another notable instance occurred in what is considered China's first #MeToo case. In October 2017, Luo Qianqian, a Ph.D. student at Beihang University, accused her professor, Chen Xiaowu, of long-term sexual harassment. The case progressed slowly until Luo contacted journalist Huang Xueqin through a sexual harassment survey. With Huang's guidance, they launched the "Hard Candy" alliance and exposed Chen's misconduct on social media on January 1, 2018. This disclosure led to widespread media attention and a petition from university professors that prompted the Ministry of Education to revoke Chen Xiaowu's "Yangtze Scholar" title on January 14, marking the onset of China's #MeToo movement. Huang Xueqin, who identifies as both a journalist and a feminist activist, was arrested in September 2021, with charges speculated to be linked to her involvement in the 2019 Hong Kong protests (AP, 2024).

In a 2018 interview, I asked Huang Xueqin whether she saw herself more as a journalist or an activist when advising Luo Qianqian and other victims. Huang stated she had not considered the distinction, feeling compelled by her journalistic resources to amplify victims' voices and raise awareness. The potential for journalists to act as social activists is feasible but has sparked ethical debates, especially in an era where social media allows editorial independence, possibly compromising objectivity. Discussions continue whether journalists should participate in or organize social movements.

Journalists are traditionally expected to maintain objectivity and impartiality, serving as information conduits rather than story participants. They are tasked with investigating, reporting facts, and providing balanced viewpoints, ensuring personal biases do not skew coverage. In contrast, activists advocate for specific causes and seek change, often with a bias toward their objectives.

Xu Chao's involvement in the Xianzi case illustrates these roles' potential overlap and conflict. Using her platform and audience to amplify Xianzi's allegations shifted her from neutrality to advocacy, which led *Caixin* to distance herself from her actions in the subsequent legal challenges. This highlights the complexities organizations face when employees adopt activist stances.

Similarly, Huang Xueqin's support of Luo Qianqian blurred the lines between journalism and activism. Her journalistic skills helped publicize Luo's story, yet her methods were more characteristic of an advocate than of a neutral reporter. Her arrest and subsequent charges underscore the risks journalists face when engaging in activism, especially in restrictive environments.

These cases underscore journalists' ethical and professional dilemmas regarding objectivity versus advocacy. Moreover, their influence and responsibilities can profoundly impact society, and engaging in activism exposes them to legal and professional risks, particularly in countries with strict media controls.

The ongoing debate on whether journalists should act as activists reflects broader discussions about the media's role in society. Journalists have more opportunities to express personal views with social media and digital platforms, complicating public perceptions of neutrality. In today's media landscape, expecting complete detachment might be unrealistic, particularly on significant social issues like sexual harassment. Nonetheless, journalists must strive to ensure their advocacy does not compromise the accuracy and fairness of their reporting (Barnard, 2018; Day, 1999; Sorce, 2021; Vine, 2017).

Journalists covering sensitive stories must carefully balance their influence and responsibilities. They must ensure that while supporting social causes, their primary duty to inform the public accurately and impartially remains intact. The evolving media landscape suggests that finding this balance will continue to be a central theme in journalism ethics and practice discussions.

Returning to the initial scenario involving Li Songwei, Xianzi acted as an activist. Besides using social media to voice her concerns, she actively sought media attention, hoping the case would continue to receive public scrutiny. Once the case moved to judicial proceedings, continuing public support became essential for activists advancing the #MeToo movement in China. For journalists, deciding to follow such cases actively tests their boundaries and reflects their commitment to gender issues and empathy for victims. I interviewed ten Chinese journalists who reported on sexual harassment; all emphasized that their engagement with the subject was driven by a clear motive to sustain the #MeToo movement in China.

"I believe in doing as much as we can. If we do not report these issues, very few will be aware. Cases like these will only increase. We have seen many setbacks in the past two years," said J14.

"We try to find the public interest behind each case. For example, with the Li Songwei case, we focused on the chaotic state of the mental health counseling industry," said J17.

The Impact and Limitation of News Media

In this chapter, I examined the complex interplay between news media and social movements in China, mainly focusing on the #MeToo movement. The role of news media in China is paradoxical, functioning as both a controlled entity and a potential facilitator of social change. Although the state's censorship apparatus tightly governs the media landscape, certain instances demonstrate that news media can indeed play a significant role in advancing public discourse on sensitive issues like sexual harassment.

While the #MeToo movement in China is not as pervasive as its global counterparts, it illustrates how digital activism can spur media coverage, bringing broader attention to the issues. Despite stringent censorship, cases that do find their way into the media spotlight tend to foster a national conversation, albeit within the confines set by the government. For example, the story of Dr. Luo Xixi, which was cautiously reported in the media, managed to ignite discussions across the nation about sexual harassment in academia.

However, the authoritarian regime's control significantly hampered the news media's potential to facilitate social change. Journalists often navigate a precarious line, balancing state directives with the professional urge to report truthfully on social issues. This balancing act sometimes pushes journalists toward activism as they seek to amplify suppressed voices within the framework of state-imposed narratives (Ginosar & Reich, 2022; Khamis, 2013).

The emergence of journalists as activists raises significant ethical questions. On the one hand, their activism can drive social change by bringing attention to issues that might otherwise remain hidden. On the other hand, the fusion of journalism and activism can compromise journalistic objectivity, leading to potential biases in reportage. This dual role requires reevaluating journalistic ethics and responsibilities in a censored media landscape.

Moreover, the state's unpredictable censorship practices add another layer of complexity. The fear of reprisals, including shutdowns or penalties, fosters an environment of self-censorship among journalists. This self-censorship dilutes the impact of digital activism, as media outlets may underreport or misreport critical issues, aligning more closely with state narratives than with journalistic integrity.

Despite these challenges, the news media's role in facilitating social change should not be underestimated. By covering sensitive issues like sexual harassment, even in a controlled manner, the press helps educate the public about the nuances of such misconduct and the legal protections available to victims. This, in turn, fosters a more informed citizenry capable of advocating for change within China's legal frameworks (Gallagher, 2006; Lin, 2024).

In China, the #MeToo movement and women's rights activism face substantial censorship, with discussions on social media curtailed and media narratives tightly controlled. The movement primarily utilizes digital platforms for mobilization and awareness. Legal frameworks have gradually evolved, with the term "sexual harassment" only recently defined in the 2020 Civil Code and subsequent amendments to the Women's Protection Law, which now specify behaviors that constitute sexual harassment and require institutions to implement preventive measures. Despite these legal strides, enforcement remains lax, and the state frequently suppresses grassroots activism. This is particularly evident in higher education, where proactive anti-harassment measures are rarely executed despite new legislation, with universities often dismissing cases on moral grounds rather than tackling systemic issues. This situation underscores the complex interaction between digital activism, legal reform, and deep-seated institutional resistance in China's handling of sexual harassment. The case of Wang Di in July 2024 exemplifies the evolving role of social media as a critical platform for victims to highlight injustices—an arena traditionally dominated by the news media. The rapid viral spread of her video and the subsequent, albeit limited, university response illuminates the changing dynamics in the management and reporting of sexual harassment cases in China. These incidents remain isolated but reveal public discontent, prompting swift government responses to widespread online engagement.

While the Chinese news media operates under considerable constraints, its potential to facilitate social change remains significant. The evolving dynamics between state control and public demand for transparency continue to shape how journalists operate. As China stands at this crossroads, the future of journalism and its impact on social movements like #MeToo warrants further exploration and understanding. The ethical implications of journalistic activism, the challenges of censorship, and the role of digital platforms in shaping public discourse are critical areas that need to be addressed to fully comprehend the potential and limitations of news media in authoritarian contexts.

References

AP. (2024). Chinese journalist who promoted #MeToo movement sentenced to 5 years in prison. *AP.* Retrieved from https://apnews.com/article/china-journalist-sentenced-metoo-huang-xuewin-73186cfeb33e8cea3bde9bf0c0b38726

Bai, Y. J., & Wang, X. C. (2021). Exclusive interview with Zhu Jun sexual harassment whistleblower: Will not back down if brought to court. *Vista Global Politics and Business Think Tan.* Retrieved from https://web.archive.org/web/20201202152330/https://v20.tp.wkread.com/index.php/WeiXin/Share/zkShare/article_id/14302/

Barnard, S. R. (2018). Tweeting# Ferguson: Mediatized fields and the new activist journalist. *New Media & Society*, *20*(7), 2252–2271.

BBC. (2021). Xianzi: The #MeToo icon China is trying to silence. *BBC*. Retrieved from https://www.bbc.com/news/world-asia-china-58629102

Caple, T. (2019). Rice bunnies in China's# MeToo: Discussion of a Feminist Movement under censorship.

Chang, F. F. (2021). Maishao enters the storm. *Huxiu.com*. Retrieved from https://web.archive.org/web/20200803122831/https://www.huxiu.com/article/269694.html

Chen, C., & Wang, X. (2020). # Metoo in China: Affordances and Constraints of Social Media Platforms. In John Jones, Michael Trice. *Platforms, protests, and the challenge of networked democracy* (pp. 253–269). Palgrave macmillan, UK.

Davidson, H. (2021). Peng Shuai: The tennis star at centre of China's biggest #MeToo allegation. *The Guardian*. Retrieved from https://www.theguardian.com/sport/2021/nov/26/peng-shuai-tennis-star-centre-china-biggest-metoo-allegation

Day, L. (1999). The journalist as citizen activist: The ethical limits of free speech. *Communication Law and Policy*, *4*(1), 1–34.

Gallagher, M. E. (2006). Mobilizing the law in China: "Informed disenchantment" and developing legal consciousness. *Law & Society Review*, *40*(4), 783–816.

Ginosar, A., & Reich, Z. (2022). Obsessive–activist journalists: A new model of journalism? *Journalism Practice*, *16*(4), 660–680.

Han, L., & Liu, Y. (2024). # metoo activism without the# MeToo hashtag: Online debates over entertainment celebrities' sex scandals in China. *Feminist Media Studies*, *24*(4), 657–674.

Khamis, S. (2013). Gendering the Arab Spring: Arab women journalists/activists, "cyberfeminism," and the sociopolitical revolution. In Cynthia Carter, Linda Steiner, Lisa McLaughlin. *The Routledge companion to media & gender* (pp. 565–575). Routledge.

Lee, F. L., Tang, G. K., & Chan, C. K. (2023). Media self-censorship in a self-censoring society: Transformation of journalist-source relationships in Hong Kong. *Journalism Studies*, *24*(12), 1539–1556.

Liao, S., & Luqiu, L. R. (2022). # MeToo in China: The dynamic of digital activism against sexual assault and harassment in higher education. *Signs: Journal of Women in Culture and Society*, *47*(3), 741–764.

Lin, J. (2024). Media coverage of domestic violence-related issues in China. *Media Asia,* 5, pp. 1–21.

Ling, Q., & Liao, S. (2020). Intellectuals debate# MeToo in China: Legitimizing feminist activism, challenging gendered myths, and reclaiming feminism. *Journal of Communication*, *70*(6), 895–916.

May, T., & Wang, Z. X. (2024). What a professor's firing shows about sexual harassment in China. *The New York Times*. Retrieved from https://www.nytimes.com/2024/07/25/world/asia/china-professor-sexual-harassment.html

Ou, L. (2021). China's first #MeToo case tests the Party. *China File*. Retrieved from https://www.chinafile.com/library/nyrb-china-archive/chinas-first-big-metoo-case-tests-party

Sorce, G. (2021). Journalist-activist boundary work in populist times: The# NazisRaus debate in German media. *Journalism Practice*, *15*(7), 894–910.

The Paper (2024). In analysis: Lawsuit sparks debate on China's therapy standards. *Six Tone*. Retrieved from https://www.sixthtone.com/news/1015275

Vine, P. (2017). When is a journalist, not a journalist?: Negotiating a new form of advocacy journalism within the environmental movement. *Pacific Journalism Review, 23*(1), 43–54.

Wu, W. (2021). *Framing# MeToo Movement in China: A content analysis of China women's news coverage* (Master's thesis, University of South Florida).

Yin, S., & Sun, Y. (2021). Intersectional digital feminism: Assessing the participation politics and impact of the MeToo movement in China. *Feminist Media Studies, 21*(7), 1176–1192.

Yuan, S. W., Qin, J. H., & Zhang, H. (2018). Prominent CCTV host accused of sexual assault. *Caixin*. Retrieved from https://www.caixinglobal.com/2018-07-28/prominent-cctv-host-accused-of-sexual-assault-101309378.html

Zeng, J. (2020). # MeToo as connective action: A study of the anti-sexual violence and anti-sexual harassment campaign on Chinese social media in 2018. *Journalism Practice, 14*(2), 171–190.

Zhang, R. X., Wang, R. Q., & Shen, F. (2018). The female intern accused Zhujun of sexual harassment. *Caixin*. Retrieved from https://web.archive.org/web/20180727103522/https://china.caixin.com/2018-07-27/101309136.html

Zhao, I. (2020). Zhou Xiaoxuan is at the forefront of China's MeToo movement, which is slowly gaining momentum. *ABC News*. Retrieved from https://www.abc.net.au/news/2020-12-17/china-metoo-movement-after-two-years-zhu-jun-xiaoxuan/12973998

3 Hong Kong

In the Age of Democratic Backsliding

The #MeToo movement in Hong Kong ignited a critical dialogue on sexual harassment following a groundbreaking revelation by Vera Lui in November 2017. Lui, a celebrated hurdler, disclosed on Facebook that she had been sexually assaulted by her coach at the tender age of 13. This disclosure catalyzed a broader societal discussion and prompted immediate action from the highest levels of government. Chief Executive Carrie Lam directed the police commissioner to thoroughly investigate, leading to the arrest and subsequent trial of Lui's coach, although he was ultimately acquitted (Su & Leung, 2017).

Lui's courage inspired a wave of disclosures across various sectors—from entertainment to politics—where individuals shared their own experiences with sexual assault. This collective bravery helped foster a sense of solidarity and spurred victims to demand accountability, not just from their assailants but also from institutions that had historically overlooked such abuses. For instance, the #ChurchToo campaign emerged as a significant force, shedding light on the transgressions within religious institutions and prompting communities to reevaluate their internal policies and cultures (Du Mez, 2019).

However, the #MeToo movement in Hong Kong has not been without its detractors. Critics argue that the movement challenges the presumption of innocence, a cornerstone of the territory's common law system. This critique mirrors sentiments expressed in Western debates over due process. Additionally, some commentators have voiced concerns that the movement could lead to misuse of social media, potentially resulting in false accusations and a dilution of genuine cases. This backlash has been compounded by a rising anti-feminist sentiment, particularly as tensions with the Chinese government escalate, influencing public and political discourse (To, 2017).

Despite these challenges, the movement has made substantive strides toward changing policy and institutional attitudes toward sexual harassment. In sports, a domain directly impacted by Lui's case, there was a marked increase in the adoption of anti-sexual harassment policies and ethical codes for coaches. However, the Equal Opportunities Commission (EOC) study in 2020 reveals that many National Sports Associations (NSA) display Codes of Conduct online but often omit detailed complaint-handling procedures

DOI: 10.4324/9781003474562-3

and protections for complainants. The EOC suggests that the NSA include comprehensive details in their anti-sexual harassment policies and effectively communicate these policies to ensure better protection and encourage reporting within official channels (EOC, 2021).

The movement also intersected with broader social issues during the 2019 anti-extradition law amendment bill protests. Allegations of police misconduct, including a disturbing incident involving an invasive strip-search of a female arrestee and sexual harassment against female journalists, sparked another wave of public outrage. Protesters co-opted the #MeToo rhetoric to highlight issues of police brutality, further integrating the movement's themes with broader political and social grievances. They rallied under the slogan "Stop Hong Kong police's use of sexual violence" after a female arrestee was allegedly strip-searched invasively by police. Outraged attendees marked "#ProtestToo" on their arms, reacting to recurrent police misconduct. Authorities defended the strict search guidelines as necessary (Creery, 2019). Surveys among female journalists who covered the protests also revealed pervasive harassment from police and government supporters (Luqiu, 2022).

The Roles of Government, Civil Society, and Media in Addressing Sexual Violence in Hong Kong

Lai (2021) summarized the collaborative model in Hong Kong, where the government, civil society, and media work together to address sexual violence. The government is responsible for penalizing sexual offenses. In Hong Kong, sexual assault can be both a criminal and civil offense. Victims can report incidents to the Hong Kong Police Force (HKPF), responsible for investigating and making arrests. Prosecutions are then processed by the Department of Justice (DOJ). For civil litigation, the Sex Discrimination Ordinance (SDO) prohibits sexual harassment in workplaces, in educational establishments, and when providing goods, services, and facilities. Victims can take their case directly to the District Court or file a complaint with the Equal Opportunity Committee and seek legal assistance. Upon receiving a complaint, the EOC facilitates conciliation or provides free legal services to the victims (Tsui, 2020).

Hong Kong had a strong civil society where scholars, activists, and NGOs played independent roles in tackling sexual violence through public education, policy advocacy, and supporting survivors. Back in 1976, victims of sexual abuse in Hong Kong had limited support, often facing stigma and public exposure through unregulated media reporting. Women pregnant from rape were even barred from legal abortion. The advancement in women's rights was lagging, prompting scholars and NGOs to take action (Lethbridge, 1980). In the 1980s, activists and NGOs launched the War on Rape campaign (Cheung, 1987). During the #MeToo movement, civil society actively pushed the police to address sexual harassment during protest movements by organizing protest rallies—a common practice in Hong Kong for advocating change and raising public attention, primarily through the news media. In the collaborative model, the press served as an independent social actor, covering sexual violence cases to raise public awareness and facilitate discussions among scholars, NGOs, critics, and stakeholders from various sectors, helping to debunk public misconceptions (Lai, 2021).

During the #MeToo movement, the Hong Kong government acted positively in this collaborative model to fulfill its role as the penalizer and preventer. The EOC actively conducts studies on the sports and higher education sectors, which is crucial for implementing new measures, such as codes of ethics on workplace sexual harassment (EOC, 2019). However, after the 2019 protest movement, the political environment in Hong Kong changed significantly, impacting this collaborative model. Although the mechanisms still exist for victims to seek justice legally, without public pressure, the government no longer acts positively in response to public demand. Chief Executive Carrie Lam rejected an independent investigation into police accused of violating human rights, including sexual harassment (Wong, 2020). With the passage and implementation of the National Security Law in 2020, when the anti-sexual violence agenda could be seen as a political challenge to authority, the government would not uphold the agenda, and civil society had almost no room to advocate change (Lai, 2021).

The shift in Hong Kong's media system marks a significant departure from its previously more liberal framework, which aligns more closely with the restrictive media environment in mainland China (Frisch et al., 2018). This transformation has profound implications for the role of news media in society, especially in addressing and discussing sensitive social issues. Historically, Hong Kong's media was known for its vibrancy and relative freedom. It allowed for investigative journalism that held power to account and facilitated a public discourse largely unfettered by governmental oversight. This environment enabled the media to play a critical role in the collaborative model of tackling different issues by raising awareness, educating the public, and pushing for policy changes. However, with the new media paradigm under the National Security Law, the press faces increased censorship and self-censorship, significantly hampering its ability to operate independently (Lee & Chan, 2010). The law's vague definitions of crimes such as subversion, secession, terrorism, and collusion with foreign forces have instilled a climate of fear among journalists. Reporting that was once considered routine investigative work can now be seen as a challenge to authority and, thus, a breach of the law. Reduced investigative reporting is a direct consequence of the fear of legal repercussions. This decrease in the depth and breadth of reporting limits public knowledge and engagement with critical social issues (Lee & Chan, 2023).

As news media outlets become more cautious about content perceived as politically sensitive, the space for public discourse shrinks. These discussions, crucial for societal change, especially in areas like sexual harassment and gender equality, are stifled. The impact on civil society is significant. News media plays a crucial role in amplifying the voices of civil society. With the news media's reduced capacity to challenge or critique government actions, civil society groups find it harder to advocate for change or rally public support (Lee, 2023). This diminishes their effectiveness in driving social and legal reforms.

Additionally, the international community's perception of Hong Kong's commitment to human rights and free speech has been negatively affected, impacting the region's credibility and potentially deterring international collaborations aimed at improving societal issues like sexual harassment. In policy-making, the news media's role is curtailed when it cannot freely report on or criticize government policies. The lack of robust media scrutiny leads to less accountability and potentially slower progress in addressing issues like sexual violence.

In this chapter, I use the orientation camps (O'Camps) at Hong Kong universities as a case study to examine whether there were differences in how the news media reported on this issue before and after the anti-extradition bill protests in 2019.

The Case of O'Camps: Why It Became a Hot Topic

In 2021, the EOC conducted a pioneering survey on sexual harassment in Hong Kong. It revealed that 17.8% of internet users and 11.8% of workers had experienced sexual harassment online and at work, respectively. Young women aged 18–34 were the most affected demographic. With over 5,000 participants, the survey demonstrated a high awareness of sexual harassment, as evidenced by an average score of 80.26 on the Sexual Harassment Awareness Index (EOC, 2022). This heightened awareness is vital for further improving the situation and enhancing the mechanisms in place, especially the government's role in penalizing and preventing such incidents. In the context of political changes in Hong Kong, the question arises: Can news media still collaborate effectively with the government and civil society? Furthermore, can the media continue to facilitate public discussions on sexual harassment? I will explore these questions using the example of anti-sexual harassment initiatives on campuses.

The EOC's comprehensive study on sexual harassment among university students in Hong Kong disclosed that 23% of students had experienced sexual harassment within the past year. However, a mere 2.5% reported these incidents to their universities. Conducted between March and April 2018, the study surveyed 14,442 students from nine universities, achieving a response rate of 14.3%. The study also included in-depth interviews and a focus group discussion with university representatives. The findings indicated that sexual harassment occurred in various settings, including on-campus, off-campus, and online, predominantly perpetrated by male classmates. The most common forms reported were sexually suggestive comments or jokes either made in the presence of or directly to the students, as well as inappropriate physical contact. Notably, many harassment cases were reported on social media platforms. Despite university efforts to combat sexual harassment, more than half of the students were unaware of their university's anti-harassment policies, and many deemed these efforts insufficient. The study underscored the need for improved sexual harassment awareness and recommended enhancing educational programs to include gender equality and relationship education starting from earlier education levels. The EOC has recommended that universities demonstrate a more substantial commitment to eliminating campus sexual harassment and improving support for victims, among other strategic recommendations, to address this pervasive issue (EOC, 2019).

Among campus sexual harassment issues, O'Camps, or orientation camps, have become a hotbed for controversy, especially starting in 2023. These camps, meant to welcome and integrate new students into university life, have come under scrutiny due to a series of sexual harassment allegations. Notably, incidents involving a fourth-year student at the Education University of Hong Kong and a second-year student at the University of Hong Kong have sparked significant public and political outcry. The student was arrested and charged with two charges of indecent assault and a third allegation of voyeurism when taking part in orientation camps (Ye, 2023). These cases have led to a renewed focus on student behavior and the responsibility of universities to safeguard their students. The Chief Executive of Hong Kong, John Lee Ka-chiu, condemned these acts as "intolerable," stressing that universities must collaborate with law enforcement to address such misconduct effectively (Lo et al., 2023).

This surge in reported incidents at O'Camps has prompted lawmakers, who typically showed little interest in the intricacies of sexual harassment issues, to question the efficacy of existing university policies. They highlighted the recurring nature of these incidents and debated the adequacy of the measures universities had implemented. The discussion underscored a growing consensus on the need for stricter oversight and enhanced moral education within university settings (Ma, 2023). As a result, various universities across Hong Kong, including the Hong Kong University of Science and Technology and the University of Hong Kong, have introduced rigorous guidelines for organizing O'Camps. These include mandatory training for camp leaders on sexual harassment prevention, pre-orientation workshops, and thorough post-event evaluations to ensure a safer environment for all participants (The Standard, 2023).

I collected news articles from Chinese newspapers in Hong Kong spanning from January 1, 2014, to June 30, 2024. Utilizing Wiserserach, I performed a keyword search for "sexual harassment" and ultimately curated a dataset of 68 stories after data cleaning. Figure 3.1 illustrates that initially, the Chinese-language newspapers did not significantly focus on sexual

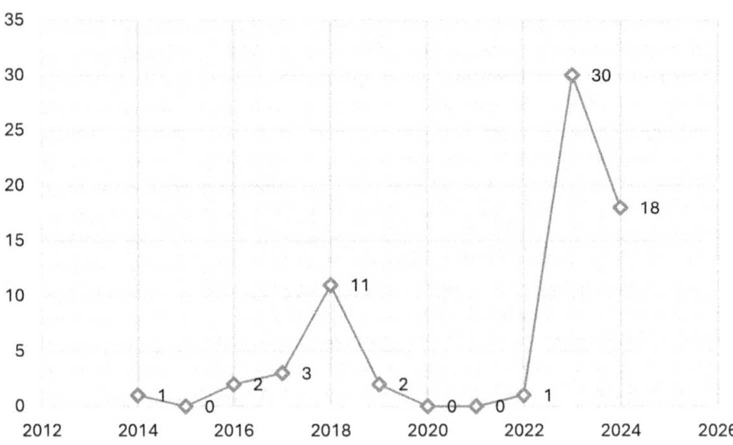

Figure 3.1 News Coverage of Sexual Harassment in University O'Camps (January 1, 2014–June 30, 2024).

harassment at university campuses, even following the publication of a study by the 3.1EOC on campus sexual harassment in 2019. Before 2019, a few incidents that occurred during orientation camps were reported. It was not until 2023 that the issue of sexual harassment at O'Camps received substantial media attention, with a noticeable increase in coverage. Due to the COVID-19 pandemic, no O'Camps were held in 2020 and 2021 as universities shifted to online teaching. Even in 2022, few O'Camps were organized due to ongoing social distancing policies, with students required to wear masks during campus gatherings.

Before 2019: The Impact of Episodic Reporting on Public Discourse Around Sexual Harassment

Coverage of sexual harassment incidents at university orientation camps increased notably in 2018, a rise linked to the global #MeToo movement that gained prominence in 2017. The movement gained significant attention in Hong Kong when Vera Liu accused a former coach of misconduct, marking the region's first widely publicized #MeToo case. Public discussions were polarized, with both supportive and skeptical voices, but these conversations undoubtedly elevated awareness about sexual harassment. This increased interest influenced the news media's agenda-setting, prompted editors to allocate more resources for in-depth coverage, and spurred journalists to seek expert interviews.

O'Camps are usually closed to outsiders and often remain underreported unless attendees share their experiences online. In 2018, three such cases surfaced on social media, drawing news media attention only after they became viral. At the Chinese University, a male student was accused of molesting a senior female student during a game. The organizers responded by alerting students via WhatsApp to "be wary of individuals with poor morals," specifically advising girls to protect themselves. Displeased with handling the incident, someone posted the details online, prompting the university to engage with the student organization responsible for the event. The university highlighted its sexual harassment complaint committee and its initiatives to educate new students, including workshops for those organizing orientation camps. The student organization intended to maintain communication with the university and involve the police if necessary.

Another incident at City University involved complaints about "pornographic" elements in games at an orientation camp, with related photos posted online. Public opinion was divided; some viewed the behavior as inappropriate, if not outright harassment, while others argued that it was acceptable if consensual, given that university students are adults. The student organization claimed the controversial activity was an impromptu addition by participants meant to enhance the event's atmosphere, carried out voluntarily. The university administration noted that they had not received any formal complaints.

At the Hong Kong University of Science and Technology, netizens shared photos alleging inappropriate activities at an orientation event. The photos depicted female students being asked to burst balloons by sitting on male students. Although the news media detailed these descriptions and included critical comments from netizens, they did not verify the authenticity of the photos. The university administration responded by clarifying that they had received no complaints or requests for help and confirmed that the photos were not from that year's activities.

In their reporting, the media extensively described games involving "pornographic" elements, but only a few outlets conducted interviews with legal experts to discuss whether such behaviors could be classified as sexual harassment and how individuals could legally protect their rights.

> Chong Yiu-kwong, a senior lecturer at the Education University and a lawyer, stated that unwelcome acts involving a sexual nature that offend, insult, or intimidate constitute sexual harassment as defined by the Sex Discrimination Ordinance. Sexual harassment is not a criminal offense and does not require a motive; even 'just playing around' can objectively constitute harassment. He mentioned that placing balloons on the chest, which is related to female sexual characteristics, can be seen as a sexual act. If the victim or other women present feel uneasy or offended, it qualifies as sexual harassment. They can file a complaint with the Equal Opportunities Commission or sue for civil damages, with compensation likely calculated in the tens of thousands of dollars.
>
> —*Apple Daily,* September 1, 2018

> Barrister Luk Wai-hung mentioned that whether a game involves sexual harassment depends on the nature of the game and the extent of physical contact. If participants know beforehand that the game involves mouth-to-mouth contact and are willing to participate, then a complaint may not be valid. However, if the format of the game changes mid-way, the participants will express their discomfort, and the others will continue regardless. It could be grounds for a sexual harassment complaint with the Equal Opportunities Commission. If someone's actions exceed the boundaries, it might even constitute indecency. He reminds students that there should be boundaries in organizing activities and they must abide by the law.
>
> —*Oriental Daily*, September 1, 2018

The episodic framing prevalent in news reporting focuses on specific events or incidents, often detailing them in isolation without providing broader context or analysis (Pan & Kosicki, 1993). This approach can simplify complex issues and focus public attention on individual moments rather than on systemic problems. This type of framing is evident in reports on university orientation activities involving questionable games. It leads to discussions that focus merely on the surface behaviors and labels for university students rather than on the severity of these behaviors, why they occur, how they can be prevented, and what systemic changes might be necessary. Therefore, the news media's reliance on episodic framing in this context does not effectively contribute to a comprehensive public discourse. Instead of fostering a more profound understanding or prompting a systemic review, it keeps the discourse superficial and reactionary, ultimately hindering the societal and institutional change needed to address such issues more effectively.

In January 2019, the EOC published its study on campus sexual harassment. Despite the study surveying nine universities across Hong Kong with 14,442 student respondents, media coverage was limited, was brief, and lacked follow-up. The reports treated this as routine news, overlooking information that warranted further investigation. For instance, a report by the *Hong Kong Economic Times* mentioned that 28 students who had experienced sexual harassment were invited for in-depth interviews. These cases included verbal harassment and, in some instances, indecent assault and attempted rape. However, when the interviewing committee offered further assistance, all were declined for personal reasons. Media could explore why victims do not report to the police or pursue further action, whether due to a lack of trust in existing mechanisms or the inadequacy of those mechanisms.

This study also asked respondents why they chose not to complain to their universities. The same article mentioned that nearly one-quarter (23%) of university students had experienced sexual harassment in the past 12 months, with 72.7% of the harassers being fellow students and 4.4% being lecturers or professors. Although 15.6% said the incidents occurred on campus, only 2.5% reported them to the university. Reasons for not reporting included believing the incident was not serious, thinking it could be resolved personally, or uncertainty about whether it qualified as sexual harassment. Despite these data, the news media needed to follow up sufficiently to maintain societal attention, which is regrettable.

Ming Pao selected a part of the study related to O'Camps and reported on a "suspected" sexual harassment incident at a City University welcome event previously covered by the news media. The report mentioned that when asked if requiring the university's prior approval could improve the situation, the EOC deemed it unfeasible. It also noted that after the EOC suspended training for students organizing O'Camps, reports of sexual harassment at these events increased, but the reasons for the suspension were not mentioned. This article chose a different angle by focusing on the survey results about students' awareness of what constitutes sexual harassment—according to the study, a quarter of the respondents failed to adequately understand sexual harassment, indicating that university students' awareness is lacking. This, too, is a news angle worth pursuing further through interviews to discuss improving students' understanding of sexual harassment, which is fundamental to mitigating campus harassment. Unfortunately, the media did not follow up on this issue either.

The deficiency in thorough and persistent reporting can be attributed to a multitude of factors. Internally, editors within news organizations may not deem the topic to possess substantial news value; externally, educational institutions often advocate for minimal media exposure, apprehensive about potential reputational harm. Consequently, this amalgamation of factors results in the media's failure to seize the opportunity to address a significant societal issue and to engage collaboratively with government entities and non-governmental organizations for improvements. Despite the EOC providing robust and reliable data through its study, the news media neglected this opportunity and did not meet their obligations as gatekeepers of information. This oversight not only represents a missed journalistic opportunity but also constitutes a disservice to the public, who depend on the news media to illuminate and champion solutions to pressing societal challenges, such as sexual harassment on university campuses.

Post-2019: Government Discourse Dominates the Reporting

Following the COVID-19 pandemic, university teaching and orientation camps resumed on campuses for the academic year 2023–2024. The first reported case of sexual harassment during an O'Camp was posted on Instagram on August 26 by an individual claiming to be a freshman at the University of Hong Kong. The post described an incident where a male student allegedly groped another freshman during the event. Due to uncertainty about the appropriate reporting channel, the incident was exposed online. On the day of the posting, the student organization responsible for the event urged the victim to file a formal complaint with them. On August 28, a spokesperson from the University of Hong Kong announced initiating an investigation. By August 29, the media had covered the incident and interviewed the police, who confirmed that a report had been filed and an investigation was underway. The outcome of this incident was briefly mentioned in a *Hong Kong Economic Journal* report on September 5, which also covered another sexual assault case at an O'Camp at the Education University. In this case, the suspect was charged with two counts of indecency and appeared in court on September 4; the case was postponed for further police investigation upon the prosecution's request, and the suspect was released on HK$5,000 cash bail until the next hearing on November 13.

On September 5, the media reported another suspected rape at an orientation event at the Education University. On September 2, a female participant posted on Instagram about a man who entered her shower and failed to apologize. Hours later, another post from the same account claimed the same individual raped another female student who participated in the O'Camp. The news report disclosed the man's surname and mentioned he was a 28-year-old student enrolled in a bridging course. The police confirmed receiving complaints from both women, but no arrests had been made. On September 4, the Education University informed all staff and students of their cooperation with the police investigation and their ongoing communication with the affected students. Additionally, the university established a dedicated team to review the operation of welcoming camps. Following the report, both the Chief Executive, John Lee, and the Education Bureau declared a zero-tolerance policy toward sexual assaults and other illegal activities in universities.

These incidents raised questions about how universities should regulate orientation camps and whether they should intervene. News media coverage continued intermittently until June 2024, unfolding in four phases. Initially, the focus was on the two cases, the responses from universities and the Education Bureau, and official guidelines. In early October, the Legislative Council's Committee on Education Affairs discussed managing university student activities and moral education, leading to various universities improving oversight of orientation activities. For instance, the Education University required student organizations to submit detailed reports on activities, and Lingnan University assigned roles such as "Anti-Bullying and Sexual Harassment Masters" to supervise events. This phase underscored the collaborative model involving the government, news media, and NGOs, with professional teacher groups and educational policy organizations actively participating in discussions and seminars. The third phase in January 2024 involved the Education Bureau reporting to the Legislative Council's Committee on Education Affairs on criminal cases involving student-led activities over the past decade.

This report was extensively covered by the media but needed in-depth analysis. The fourth phase focused on discussions by the Legislative Council's Committee on Political Affairs concerning sexual harassment at university orientation camps, highlighting the EOC's positive response to recommendations made to universities. Around this time, the news media also reported on new requirements for orientation camps imposed by some universities, such as Lingnan University's prohibition of student organizations using the terms "orientation camp" and "orientation activities."

News media reporting was notably reactive rather than proactive throughout these stages, beginning coverage only after university responses or police involvement were confirmed. This passive approach continued through discussions in the Legislative Council, with the media shying away from addressing the crucial role of the police in managing campus sexual harassment issues. A significant oversight emerged in July when a suspect previously involved in an indecency case and implicated in a rape case at the Education University was not immediately arrested due to insufficient evidence. This highlighted a potential gap in the police's approach to handling such cases, suggesting a need for specialized training and dedicated units similar to those in the United States, indicated by the experts and scholars, which could enhance the handling of sexual violence cases and encourage more victims to come forward (Ng & Cheng, 2018). In 2018, the news media actively engaged in discussions regarding how police could enhance their approach to handling cases of sexual violence, highlighting several deficiencies in their methods. However, during the 2023–2024 discourse concerning the mitigation of sexual violence on university campuses, the critical role of the police as primary enforcers of the law and initial gatekeepers in the criminal justice process to secure justice for victims conspicuously diminished on news media.

Underreporting and Oversight

In the reporting and handling of sexual harassment issues during university orientation camps in Hong Kong, the media's role reflects both collaboration and challenges across various sectors. Before the 2019 Anti-Extradition Law Amendment Bill Movement, government bodies, from the Education Bureau to the Legislative Council, paid scant attention to sexual harassment incidents at university orientation camps. This lack of focus was tied to respect for university and student autonomy. However, during the same period, there were proactive initiatives, notably a campus sexual harassment study conducted in 2018, which resonated with the global #MeToo movement's influence in Hong Kong. Unfortunately, there is much room for improvement in the coverage of this issue in Hong Kong news media.

After the 2019 movement, government and Legislative Council interventions demonstrated an increased focus on the governance of higher education institutions and student activities. For example, the Education Bureau required universities to submit reports on student activities and proposed improvements in managing orientation camps, reflecting a commitment to strengthening campus management. Legislative discussions and demands also drove further policy development and revision. Positively, these efforts helped in tackling sexual violence on campuses. However, they also risked overcorrecting by undermining student autonomy, complicating the already challenging operation of student organizations, and potentially damaging relationships between university administrations and students due to the enforced perception of a strict parental governance role. The pressure from the Legislative Council and government also impacted university autonomy.

In this reporting process, the news media appeared relatively passive. Initial reports often relied on official announcements from universities or the government, needing more proactive investigative efforts. While the media did provide some follow-up coverage, it generally fell short in terms of analysis and depth. Notably, there was an insufficient exploration of the police's role and efficiency in handling sexual harassment cases, failing to reveal systemic issues adequately. Instead, the voices featured in reports were predominantly those of officials and legislators, needing more diverse perspectives from society, which hindered practical public discourse and the development of better approaches to addressing the issues. Ideally, news organizations should strengthen their independent investigations and report on campus sexual harassment, provide more comprehensive analyses, and offer constructive criticism of related policies and measures. This would help identify the root causes of the issues and promote solutions that benefit all parties, especially in protecting student rights and enhancing public confidence in the capabilities of police and educational institutions to handle such matters.

References

Cheung, F. (1987). Changing attitudes: The war-on-rape campaign. *Bulletin of the Hong Kong Psychological Society*, *19*(20), 41–48.

Creery, J. (2019). #ProtestToo: Hongkongers adopt anti-sexual harassment rallying cry in response to police assault allegations. *Hong Kong Free Press*. Retrieved from https://hongkongfp.com/2019/08/29/protesttoo-hongkongers-adopt-anti-sexual-harassment-rallying-cry-response-police-assault-allegations/

Du Mez, K. (2019). When #ChurchToo goes global. *Patheos*. Retrieved from https://www.patheos.com/blogs/anxiousbench/2019/03/when-churchtoo-goes-global/

EOC. (2019). Break the silence: Territory-wide study on sexual harassment of university students in Hong Kong. *Equal Opportunity Committee*. Retrieved from https://www.eoc.org.hk/eoc/Upload/ResearchReport/SH2018/ENG/SH%20University%20Report_ENG_Full%20Report.pdf

EOC. (2021). Report on the formulation of anti-sexual harassment policy among national sports association in Hong Kong 2020. *The Equal Opportunity Committee*. Retrieved from https://www.eoc.org.hk/compass/wp-content/uploads/2021/08/Report-on-the-Formulation-of-Anti-Sexual-Harassment-Policy-among-National-Sports-Association-in-Hong-Kong-2020-ENG.pdf

EOC. (2022). EOC releases findings of the first-ever territory-wide representative survey on sexual harassment in Hong Kong. *Equal Opportunity Committee*. Retrieved from https://www.eoc.org.hk/en/PressRelease/Detail/18479

Frisch, N., Belair-Gagnon, V., & Agur, C. (2018). Media capture with Chinese characteristics: Changing patterns in Hong Kong's news media system. *Journalism*, *19*(8), 1165–1181.

Lai, R. Y. (2021). From# MeToo to# ProtestToo: How a feminist movement converged with a pro-democracy protest in Hong Kong. *Politics & Gender*, *17*(3), 500–507.

Lee, F. (2023). Beyond self-censorship: Hong Kong's journalistic risk culture under the national security law. *The China Journal*, *90*(1), 129–153.

Lee, F. L., & Chan, C. K. (2023). Legalization of press control under democratic backsliding: The case of post-national security law Hong Kong. *Media, Culture & Society*, *45*(5), 916–931.

Lee, F. L., & Chan, J. M. (2010). *Media, social mobilization and mass protests in post-colonial Hong Kong: The power of a critical event*. Routledge.

Lethbridge, H. (1980). Rape, reform, and feminism in Hong Kong. *Hong Kong Law Journal*, *10*, 260.

Lo, C., Kong, H., & Lo, H. Y. (2023). Hong Kong police investigating sex assault case at second university, while city leader warns varsities to instil discipline. *South China Morning Post*. Retrieved from https://www.scmp.com/news/hong-kong/law-and-crime/article/3233402/hong-kong-police-launch-probe-rape-allegation-education-university-orientation-camp

Luqiu, L. R. (2022). Female journalists covering the Hong Kong protests confront ambivalent sexism on the street and in the newsroom. *Feminist Media Studies*, *22*(3), 679–697.

Ma, J. (2023). Hong Kong lawmakers demand stricter controls on university orientation camps after series of sex assault allegations by students. *South China Morning Post*. Retrieved from https://www.scmp.com/news/hong-kong/education/article/3237125/hong-kong-lawmakers-demand-stricter-controls-university-orientation-camps-after-series-sex-assault

Ng, W. Y., & Cheng, C. Y. (2018). Sexual assault: Why the silence? Not reporting to police prevents evidence collection and medical examination, facing court only to be humiliated again. *Ming Pao Weekly*. Retrieved from https://www.mpweekly.com/culture/cu0001/%e6%80%a7%e4%be%b5-%e6%80%a7%e9%a8%b7%e6%93%be-%e5%bc%b7%e5%a7%a6-78663

Pan, Z., & Kosicki, G. M. (1993). Framing analysis: An approach to news discourse. *Political Communication*, *10*(1), 55–75.

The Standard. (2023). Universities' guidelines on organizing orientation camps were released in light of recent scandals. *The Standard*. Retrieved from https://www.thestandard.com.hk/breaking-news/section/4/207903/Universities'-guidelines-on-organizing-orientation-camps-revealed-in-light-of-recent-scandals

Su, X. Q., & Leung, C. (2017). Hong Kong hurdler Vera Lui's claim that a coach sexually assaulted her when she was 13 sparks outcry, police probe. *South China*

Morning Post. Retrieved from https://www.scmp.com/news/hong-kong/law-crime/article/2122203/coach-sexually-assaulted-her-when-she-was-13-hong-kong

To, D. (2017). Hong Kong's 'MeToo campaign' faces severe backlash. *TRT World.* Retrieved from https://www.trtworld.com/asia/hong-kong-s-me-too-campaign-faces-severe-backlash-14852

Tsui, C. Y. (2020). Judging the Oonline Jjudges: The Ttwo# MeToo Ccases in Hong Kong. *FACTA UNIVERSITATIS-Philosophy, Sociology, Psychology and History, 19*(3), 241–255.

Wong, T. K. (2020). Hong Kong protests: Carrie Lam says no once again to independent police inquiry. *South China Morning Post.* Retrieved from https://www.scmp.com/yp/discover/news/hong-kong/article/3070562/hong-kong-protests-carrie-lam-says-no-once-again

Ye, L. (2023). University O'Camps went wrong. *Varsity.* Retrieved from https://varsity.com.cuhk.edu.hk/index.php/2023/12/university-ocamps-went-wrong/

4 Taiwan

Assessing the Gatekeeper Role of News Media in #MeToo Movement: Successes and Shortcomings

In 2017, as the #MeToo movement gained global momentum, Taiwan stood as a notable exception. Despite its reputation as a liberal democracy and one of the most gender-equal societies in Asia—evidenced by legal same-sex marriage, a high ratio of women in political roles, and a female president not born into a political dynasty—it was conspicuously absent from the global and regional #MeToo narratives. This gap might be attributed to a deficiency in high-quality journalism within Taiwan, which could have played a critical role in fostering this movement (Chen & Huang, 2023).

The dynamics of speaking out against sexual misconduct are significantly influenced by both the quality of media and its awareness of gender issues. The emergence of the #MeToo movement, although it was considered started from social media by using hashtags and mobile people all over the world, was heavily reliant on investigative journalism, as seen with pivotal exposés by the *New York Times* and *the New Yorker*, which substantiated the claims of the initial accusers. This kind of journalism was critical in giving a voice to those who might otherwise have remained silent.

Examining News Media's Role in Taiwan's #MeToo Discourse

Despite Taiwan's democratic status, which includes total freedom of the press, the quality of its media has been a persistent issue, affecting the country's democratic health. According to Fuchs (2014), this concern has long been recognized. A 2019 survey highlighted this problem, revealing that nearly 96% of respondents felt the Taiwanese media failed adequately in fact-checking and verification processes (Maxon, 2019). The inability of mainstream media to ensure due process in validating a victim's claim makes speaking out a potentially perilous act, especially for high-profile women.

Research by Tsai and Su (2016) points to a persistent issue in Taiwanese journalism: the perpetuation of rape myths, even as legal systems evolve to protect victims' privacy better and acknowledge their trauma. The study compared ten years of sexual assault reporting before and after the entry of *Apple*

DOI: 10.4324/9781003474562-4

Daily into the Taiwanese market in 2003. They found that the portrayal of perpetrators as monstrous and the victim narratives often emphasized power imbalances, potentially shaping new public perceptions under a market-driven media landscape. Reports on sexual assault frequently propagate rape myths by emphasizing the perpetrator's position of power and the victim's vulnerability. This approach reinforces stereotypes that only certain types of individuals can be victims or perpetrators of sexual assaults.

Moreover, the use of terms like "rape" and "sexual assault," which carry legal and cultural connotations, often come with solid gender and power dynamics that might not suitably describe all types of sexual offenses. News media outlets also show a tendency to cover controversial or sensational sexual assault cases involving celebrities or powerful institutions, often ignoring more common but less "dramatic" cases. To address these issues, it is crucial to enhance the sensitivity and understanding of journalists and news editors regarding gender issues. Specialized training can help media professionals appreciate the diversity and complexity of sexual assault cases. Additionally, encouraging the use of neutral and precise language in reporting can help avoid terms that carry strong gender biases or stereotypes. News media should strive to provide a more comprehensive perspective that includes reporting on sexual assault cases involving less heard groups in society, such as males and non-binary individuals. Moreover, news media outlets must recognize their role in shaping public consciousness and societal attitudes and should avoid unconsciously exacerbating gender inequality or causing secondary harm to victims.

A notable incident during the peak of the global #MeToo movement involved a senior female journalist who, through a Facebook post, accused a current minister of past sexual harassment. Although the politician remained unnamed and the president supported an investigation, there was no follow-up from the news media, and the issue faded without further exploration or disclosure of investigation details. This incident underscores the challenges within Taiwan's news media landscape in handling such sensitive issues. This also discourages others from speaking out; no victims spoke out after the news media reported this case. However, the #MeToo movement still positively impacted journalism in Taiwan, which increased the quality of journalism.

Wang (2021) analyzed the impact of the #MeToo movement on Taiwanese media by reviewing a decade of sexual harassment coverage in the *United Daily News*. Before the #MeToo movement, incidents of sexual harassment reported in the media were most frequently said to occur in public places, followed by workplaces. However, post-#MeToo, the trend reversed, with most reports focusing on workplace harassment. This shift likely reflects the increased willingness of women to come forward with their experiences of workplace harassment following the movement's rise. The spotlight on the entertainment industry, particularly on actresses who have been vocal about their experiences, has intensified media coverage of sexual harassment in this sector. As public figures, entertainers naturally attract more media attention, contributing to a surge in related news coverage. An exciting change was noted in the media post-#MeToo in the reporting details. Before the movement, descriptions of harassment tended to be detailed. After the movement, reports have shown a significant reduction in detailed harassment descriptions. This trend might be seen as positive as it avoids retraumatizing victims and does not perpetuate rape myths by sensationalizing the details of the harassment. Despite these positive changes, a notable discrepancy exists between the actual number and news media reports. This discrepancy suggests that news outlets need to consciously increase their coverage of sexual harassment to reflect reality more accurately. Such efforts will ensure that the media does not underreport or misrepresent the scope and nature of sexual harassment, which is crucial for ongoing public education and awareness.

Though delayed, the response to the #MeToo movement in Taiwan reflects the complex interplay of cultural nuances with the transformative power of media and social platforms. By incorporating societal issues into its narratives, dramas like "*Wave Makers,*" broadcast on *Netflix* in 2023, played a critical role in mobilizing public sentiment and encouraging victims to voice their experiences. The shared stories on social media and the engagement with traditional news outlets led to significant momentum within the movement, pushing the societal shift toward addressing and rectifying issues of sexual harassment and enhancing gender-based equity.

The drama "*Wave Makers*," which delved into themes of sexual assault and its concealment within a political context, resonated deeply, sparking a more assertive response from the Taiwanese public. Social media platforms, especially Facebook, became arenas for discourse, where victims shared extensive and detailed accounts of their experiences. In turn, accused perpetrators increasingly used these platforms, rather than traditional news outlets, to deny the allegations and defend themselves. Public sentiment shifted noticeably; victims' accounts were more readily accepted, while denials from the accused were met with skepticism, even without extensive news media coverage. This shift mirrored a rise in gender awareness and facilitated a more prominent public discussion about sexual harassment.

The recent evolution of the #MeToo movement in Taiwan is distinguished primarily by victims' preference to disseminate their narratives via social media as opposed to conventional outlets like press conferences or direct engagements with the media, seeking broader exposure (Feng, 2023). These online disclosures have catalyzed extensive societal discussions, consequently elevating these issues to matters of journalistic interest and leading to their frequent coverage. According to gatekeeper theory, the role of traditional news media in this context is pivotal as it not only disseminates information but also curates it to ensure balanced reporting, thereby mitigating premature judgments against the accused found commonly in online platforms (Mulupi & Blumell, 2023; Shoemaker & Vos, 2009). Furthermore, media coverage broadens the scope of public discourse from individual incidents to systemic flaws, thereby catalyzing contemplation on preventative strategies and potentially prompting policy reforms (Leifermann, 2018; McCombs & Shaw, 1972). Media participation also helps mitigate secondary victimization by providing a contextual understanding that challenges the stereotype of the "perfect victim." (Andersen, 2017). As gatekeepers, journalists hold the capacity to encourage reticent victims to voice their stories, thereby illustrating that these occurrences are not mere anomalies. However, the efficacy of this role depends on the media's commitment to high-quality journalism and avoidance of reinforcing rape myths. After the 2018 international #MeToo movement, Taiwan has seen an improvement in the quality of media reporting.

Yet, some scholars argue that the media has inadequately fulfilled its gatekeeping function in the recent wave, with public awareness instead playing a more decisive and constructive role (Chen & Huang, 2023). They have compared the performances of Taiwanese and American news media during the MeToo movement. They pointed out that since the end of May 2023, Taiwan's MeToo movement—occurring six years after America's—has been completely driven, dominated, and sustained by social media to tackle issues of sexual assault, harassment, and bullying in public spaces. They noted that traditional news media organizations, such as newspapers, magazines, and television, have merely followed the accusers' and the accused's posts on social media without conducting any independent investigations or producing comprehensive reports. According to these scholars, Taiwan's #MeToo has not seen proactive efforts from mainstream media to organize and present victims' testimonies as a collective challenge to power and institutions. Instead, the news media have only passively relayed social media posts, marking a distinct difference from America's #MeToo movement. Furthermore, these scholars criticized the type of coverage, often referred to as horse race coverage, which essentially reduces the victims—who bravely speak out on social media, risking personal exposure and using their pain as a bond of trust to publicly discuss their trauma of sexual harassment and assault in work or educational settings—to mere subjects of basic facts and progress reports (5W1H: who, what, when, where, why, and how), without engaging in deeper discussions on the broader social, cultural, or legal implications (Chen, 2023).

This situation raises questions: In light of the evolving dynamics of the #MeToo movement in Taiwan, how effective are traditional news media in fulfilling their gatekeeper role in the fight against sexual violence, considering the rising influence of social media in shaping public discourse and awareness?

Methodology

This study employed qualitative research methods to delve into the dynamics of media reporting on the recent #MeToo wave in Taiwan. In-depth interviews were conducted with a purposive sample consisting of 11 journalists (3 males and 8 females) who covered #MeToo cases and 5 victims of sexual harassment who had used social media platforms to share their experiences. These interviews were held in Taipei between January and March 2024, each lasting 35–50 minutes. To protect the interviewees' identity, all the quotations use numbers.

A semi-structured interview format was utilized, allowing the exploration of the journalistic process from the perspective of news production. This approach facilitated an examination of the criteria journalists employed in their reporting, encompassing their personal ethical codes, the editorial policies of the media outlets for which they worked, and the dynamics between journalists and editors. In addition to examining the journalists' perspectives, the study focused on the victims' experiences as media consumers. It explored their perceptions of the journalists' roles and performances during their interactions and their opinions on the impact of news coverage on society.

This study utilized critical discourse analysis (CDA) to examine the interview transcripts, thereby deepening our understanding of the interactions between media reporting and the responses of victims in the context of Taiwan's #MeToo movement. The method entailed thoroughly examining language patterns within the interviews to reveal underlying power dynamics, ideologies, and the structural aspects of newsrooms, all of which shape journalistic practices and influence victims' perceptions. The transcripts were initially read in their entirety to grasp the prevalent discourse comprehensively. This analytical approach yielded crucial insights into how discourse constructs and perpetuates specific narratives and ideologies, highlighting the role of news media as a gatekeeper and its significant impact on societal responses.

Internal Dynamics and External Influences in Newsroom Agenda-Setting

In the complex news production ecosystem, news media's agenda-setting function is multifaceted and influenced by various internal and external factors. Within the newsroom, journalists primarily gather, report, and write news stories, driven by their professional judgment and the editorial direction news editors provide. Editors play a pivotal role in shaping the news agenda by deciding which stories are published, their prominence, and the angle from which they are approached (Peiser, 2000). News media owners' overarching strategic goals and business interests often guide this decision-making process, which may indirectly influence content to align with broader corporate or political objectives (Guo & Vargo, 2015).

Beyond the internal dynamics, external influences significantly impact agenda-setting. Audiences, for instance, are powerful; their preferences, feedback, and engagement metrics often drive content strategy, pushing media outlets to favor topics that generate higher viewership or reader engagement (Coleman et al., 2009). Politicians and government entities also play a role through direct communication with journalists and editors or, more subtly, via the broader political climate and regulatory environment (Majone, 2006). The interplay between these elements—journalistic ethics, editorial policies, corporate interests, audience demands, and political pressures—shapes the news that the public ultimately consumes, highlighting the complex balance of power and responsibility in the news media's role as a gatekeeper and agenda-setter (Harrison, 2009).

During the 2023 #MeToo movement in Taiwan, increased coverage by news outlets was heavily influenced by the vibrant discussions on social media. Journalists commonly prioritize cases involving prominent individuals since public figures are deemed more relevant and newsworthy. This approach aligns with traditional news values emphasizing proximity as a key factor for newsworthiness. However, such a focus can result in polarized reporting, heightening public interest while potentially causing the public to either overlook the core issues or feel disengaged from the incidents. Sensationalism was particularly notable following the incident involving Taiwanese celebrity Micky Huang, where media reports became more sensationalized and gossipy. Despite this, many journalists and media outlets strive to initiate discussions based on the thematic essence of the #MeToo movement, aiming to foster deeper societal engagement.

> We start from the issue, researching whether there are similar trends across cases or identifying underlying social issues, such as legal deficiencies or structural imbalances. Based on these findings, we establish a reporting framework and interview individuals who have encountered similar challenges. We focus less on daily news and more on comprehensive, in-depth reporting. Identifying a trend is essential before selecting and reporting on cases that exemplify the identified theme,

explained interviewee J1.

Interviewee J4 noted,

> During our coverage of the #MeToo movement, we produced several articles, each centered on a different theme. For example, some addressed issues within educational settings, leading us to choose cases involving students or school staff. Similarly, we selected cases that resonated with the specific theme when covering workplace issues.

To enhance their reporting, journalists have invested in developing narratives that connect individual stories to broader social realities, thus providing a richer, more contextual understanding of each case. This method involves significant background research, long-term engagement with subjects, and collaboration among various stakeholders, including activists, legal experts, and other journalists. Such depth is critical in portraying the complexities of sexual misconduct and the systemic barriers that victims face. However, the need for thorough verification and interviewing can conflict with the demand for timely reporting, as interviewee J2 described:

> Initially, my supervisor directed us to concentrate on topics related to the #MeToo movement. As these topics are time-intensive, my boss later questioned whether we were overly focused on the #MeToo theme, especially with upcoming elections, suggesting a shift towards election coverage. However, I believe it's crucial to persist with these topics, provided there is institutional support.

One distinctive aspect of the #MeToo movement is that victims seek justice outside conventional systems, actively sharing their experiences through news and social media to broaden the discourse. Consequently, the ongoing focus of news media is essential for the growth and evolution of the movement (Choi, 2018). The pursuit of timeliness leads to a lack of depth in reporting as there isn't enough time to track and analyze hot social issues. Moreover, in a competitive media market, media lack the courage to continue providing resources and space for new topics when they emerge. This also reflects that many media outlets are ceding their agenda-setting power, no longer prioritizing news importance and social responsibility but instead allowing social media and pre-scheduled news events, like elections, to become the ultimate agenda-setters, and news media partially gave up their role as the gatekeeper.

Building Trust and Protecting Privacy in Interviews about Sexual Violence

In the sensitive and intricate realm of journalism, reporting on sexual violence is fraught with challenges, particularly when it comes to securing interviews with victims. These individuals often hesitate due to concerns over privacy and the distress associated with recounting traumatic events. The fear of identity exposure and the daunting prospect of a face-to-face conversation with a stranger can make formal media interviews more intimidating than sharing experiences on social media or through written narratives.

To address these initial hurdles, journalists emphasize the importance of building trust. This often involves using intermediaries known to the interviewees to create a comfortable and respectful communication environment. One journalist among the interviewees, J8 described their approach to making initial contact, highlighting the role of familiarity and trust:

> At the beginning of our selection process, we choose people we already know or use an intermediary trusted by the other party. Having such an intermediary makes it easier to establish a trust relationship.

Once trust is established, setting the framework for the interview is critical. Journalists adopt non-aggressive interview techniques and offer flexible communication methods to accommodate the needs and comfort levels of the interviewees. A journalist among the interviewees, referred to as J11, outlined their thoughtful approach:

> When I arrange interviews, I clearly state our purpose in doing this report. Since I'm aware it involves trauma, I tell them that the interview method will accommodate their feelings. We can conduct it over the phone or even in writing, and they can refuse to answer any uncomfortable questions.

Visual elements like photographs can enhance the credibility of a story, but they also require sensitive handling. Interviewee J9 explained their method to ensure respectful treatment of such sensitive content:

> For some reports, we need photographs because they lend credibility to the story. We communicate with the other party in advance and explain how we will present the photos. Whether it's text or photos, it's important to actively inform them about the final presentation to reassure them that their story is being handled respectfully.

The presence of a trusted intermediary is crucial, especially for male journalists interviewing female victims, as one interviewee J1 noted:

> Having an intermediary whom the interviewee trusts completely is crucial during the interview process. As a male journalist, I find it more challenging to discuss certain topics with female victims. Therefore, having a mediator of the same gender, or a friend or family member present, can make them feel more at ease.

Journalists also prepare mentally for the possibility of interview refusals, prioritizing the mental health of the victims over the completion of the interview. Interviewee J5 shared their perspective:

> I adopt a non-aggressive approach and mentally prepare for the possibility that they may ultimately refuse the interview. Their mental health is our top priority, and we don't want to pressure them to secure an interview.

The ethical handling of interviews is paramount. Journalists ensure the anonymity and consent of their subjects, showing drafts before publication to avoid retraumatization. This practice, while not routine in many news organizations, is crucial to maintaining trust and integrity in reporting on such sensitive issues. Interviewee J2 reflected on this practice:

> In the end, we showed the completed manuscript to our six interviewees to confirm their willingness to publish it. They reacted positively, feeling that our report accurately reflected their true feelings. We were concerned about causing secondary harm, but instead, our interviewees felt empowered because the report was truthful.

Finally, maintaining the anonymity of the interviewees is a primary concern to prevent further harm. Interviewee J10 highlighted their protective measures:

> In the process of writing the report, my primary concern was to ensure that the interviewees could not be identified to prevent further harm. So, before publishing, I showed them the parts of the manuscript that described their experiences and told them, 'If you feel there are parts that might make you recognizable, tell me, and I will modify or even remove them.'

Through these practices, journalists strive to balance sensitivity and thoroughness in reporting on sexual violence, a testament to the evolving nature of ethical journalism. In the complex and sensitive field of journalism, reporting on sexual violence involves numerous challenges, primarily in securing interviews with victims, who may hesitate due to concerns over privacy and the distress of recounting traumatic events. Journalists emphasize the importance of building trust, often using intermediaries known to the interviewees, to facilitate a comfortable and respectful communication environment. They adopt non-aggressive interview techniques, offer flexible communication methods, and prepare for the possibility of interview refusals, prioritizing the mental health of the victims. The ethical handling of interviews is critical; journalists ensure the anonymity and consent of their subjects, showing drafts before publication to avoid retraumatization—a practice not routine in many news organizations, raising questions about whether journalists can maintain a balance or may appear biased toward the victims.

Journalistic Strategies in Reporting

Fact-checking in the context of reporting sexual violence, particularly during the #MeToo movement, presents unique and substantial challenges. The time lag between the incident and reporting is a major hurdle. Many cases of sexual violence are reported several years after the incident. This delay can be due to various reasons, including trauma, fear of retribution, or the victim's uncertainty about how their allegations might be received. Over time, physical evidence is lost, and memories can fade or become distorted, making it challenging for journalists to verify the facts. Sexual violence often occurs in private settings without witnesses. This isolation means that there are rarely any third-party accounts to corroborate the stories of the victim and the accused, which is a standard method in journalism for verifying claims.

Moreover, the psychological impact on victims can affect their memory and narrative coherence. Traumatic memories can be fragmented and non-linear, which sometimes leads to inconsistencies in a victim's account of events. While understandable from a psychological perspective, these inconsistencies can be problematic for journalists aiming to present a coherent and fact-checked story (Blumell & Huemmer, 2021).

Victims may be reluctant to come forward due to fear of social stigma or victim-blaming, which can complicate the fact-checking process. The fear of not being believed or of facing retaliation can lead to vague or incomplete initial accounts, which makes verifying the details more difficult. The #MeToo movement has been heavily influenced by social media, where victims often first share their experiences. While these platforms can amplify voices that might otherwise go unheard, they also complicate fact-checking as the spread of information is rapid and only sometimes subject to prior verification. Journalists must navigate these waters carefully, distinguishing between viral allegations and those with a substantiated basis.

Reporting on sexual violence involves navigating complex legal and ethical landscapes. Journalists must ensure their reporting does not prejudice legal proceedings or unjustly harm the reputations of those involved. This requirement for careful, sensitive reporting can slow down the fact-checking process and place a high burden on journalists to get their facts right without infringing on the rights of either party. In many cases, the accused may be in a position of power, adding an additional layer of complexity. Institutions may have vested interests in protecting their reputation and influential figures, which can lead to a lack of cooperation with journalists seeking to uncover the truth, thereby hindering thorough fact-checking. Both journalists and their audiences bring their biases to the stories they tell and consume. Recognizing and overcoming these biases is critical but challenging in ensuring accurate and unbiased reporting.

These challenges highlight the delicate balance journalists must maintain between empathy for victims and rigorous adherence to journalistic standards of accuracy and fairness. The #MeToo movement, by bringing these stories to the forefront, has highlighted not only the prevalence of sexual violence but also the critical need for robust, sensitive, and ethical journalism in this area. A common method used within the industry involves interviewing multiple victims and ensuring that these individuals have not had contact with each other. By comparing the details described by all interviewees, patterns of the perpetrator's behavior often emerge, corroborating the victims' accusations.

However, reality often needs to catch up to this ideal. At such times, whether to proceed with the report or abandon it becomes a decision journalists must make. Interviewee J4 mentioned that their approach involves removing unverifiable details from their reports.

> I find this quite challenging, similar to the issues faced in subsequent legal proceedings related to sexual harassment and assault, where it is difficult to produce evidence or verify claims. When interviewing the parties involved, it is hard to validate each detail they provide to determine its accuracy or occurrence. My approach is to initially trust the interviewees, not treating their statements as deliberate lies. I encourage them to elaborate or ask more questions if something seems vague or uncertain. However, it's hard to say whether sympathy for the interviewee might lead to bias since cognitive bias can be difficult to detect.

Interviewee J2's approach involves online research, comparing the current statements of the individuals involved with their past statements to assess credibility.

> Often, these incidents happened nine or ten years ago, involving powerful individuals, making the victims uncertain or afraid to speak openly for fear of impacting their future. Yet, these issues continue to trouble them, leading them to describe their experiences vaguely on social media occasionally. I find these posts to be valuable evidence.

Interviewee J10, aiming to avoid errors and legal repercussions for their media outlet, adheres to a principle of only writing about cases that have gone through judicial procedures.

> I feel safer writing about cases with court verdicts, decisions to prosecute, or not. These have been investigated, not relying solely on one person's statement. With #Metoo cases, it's often a matter of he said, she said, which can seem arbitrary. Suppose the case has entered the judicial system. In that case, I feel somewhat more assured as you can at least discuss what the judicial investigation found, and even if there's no prosecution, you can still report that such a case occurred but was not pursued due to insufficient evidence.

Interviewee J8 noted that working for an organization with strict verification requirements makes their interviewing process easier. "Our work rules require that in addition to interviewing the main subject, I must speak with at least three to five other people, as necessary. This is a fundamental part of our job."

Journalists face significant challenges when reporting on cases of sexual violence, especially in verifying the accuracy of details from incidents that may have occurred years ago and where evidence is scarce. The practice of interviewing multiple unrelated victims to establish behavior patterns is expected but not always possible. Journalists employ various strategies to manage these challenges, including conducting thorough online research and only reporting on cases that have undergone judicial scrutiny to avoid legal risks and ensure the reliability of their reports. These practices underscore the critical balance between empathy and objectivity needed to report on sensitive issues such as sexual violence responsibly.

Victims' Perspectives on Sensitivity and Accuracy in Reporting

As victims are interviewed, how do they perceive the journalists' performance, and what are their expectations of them? The interviewed journalists all said they strive earnestly to build trust with the victims they interviewed. However, from the victims' perspective, what actions and words from the journalists can help them lower their guard? From the perspective of journalistic ethics, if journalists overly accommodate victims they interviewed to build trust, could such compromises prevent them from remaining neutral?

Interviewee V1 detailed how she decided to accept the journalist's interview. After a week of careful consideration, she agreed to the interview for two main reasons. First, although she had already shared her story anonymously on social media, she is not a celebrity, so her post received little attention. By accepting a media interview, she believed her ordeal could reach a wider audience, potentially leading to public condemnation of the perpetrator. She agreed to the interview because the journalist was acquainted with her husband, who had communicated with the journalist before making the introduction, deeming the journalist trustworthy.

> Throughout the interview, what struck me the most was realizing that you can't just say whatever you want in front of the media. Some statements, if reported, could be too vague and potentially mislead the readers, which would be to my disadvantage. The journalist informed me of this and promised to make some modifications. This was the first time I realized that being too frank with journalists could be problematic. After understanding this, I recognized how unfamiliar I was with the media and needed to learn how to interact with them properly. So, I am very grateful to this journalist.

As victims, once trust is established with a journalist, they often develop expectations beyond the journalist's duty. When these expectations are not met, it can diminish their confidence in the journalist. As interviewee V2 noted,

> The journalist was introduced by a friend. After the interview, during our interactions, I wasn't sure if the journalist truly understood the victim's state. For instance, the day I received a subpoena and posted about it on social media, the journalist's first reaction was not to show concern but to send me a message asking for an interview. This made me feel that the journalist did not understand my situation, affecting the trust level.

The above two examples highlight the same issue: journalists must consider which principles to maintain and what attitude to adopt when communicating with interviewees. In the first example, the journalist's proactive modification of some interview content can prevent secondary harm to the victim. Still, such changes could deprive readers of the information needed to form their judgments or make the report too biased. This is something that media outlets, as gatekeepers, need to consider. In the second example, how a journalist interacts with a victim of sexual violence, showing empathy and understanding of the victim's psychological state is also a professional requirement for journalists. This necessitates that news organizations provide sufficient training to journalists, making them aware of the psychological needs of interviewees.

Interviewee V4 expressed,

> One important gesture is when a journalist starts by saying, 'If you feel uncomfortable with this question, you can tell me, and you don't have to answer.' If a journalist says this, I feel that the journalist and the media are more friendly because, at the very least, they let you know you have the right to refuse to answer the question. Also, you can tell them, 'This question makes me uncomfortable.' This makes me feel safe.

The interviewed journalists all stated that this is a fundamental step in building trust. Still, it also raises the question of how to ask questions in a way that makes the interviewee less uncomfortable and more willing to share. This interviewing skill, especially in cases of targeted violence, also requires specific guidelines.

How news reports are presented significantly impacts public perception of victims' experiences, a fact highlighted by the dissatisfaction expressed by four out of five interviewees regarding the final presentation of their stories. Interviewee V1 criticized the media's strategy of using sensational labels to grab attention:

> The media chooses some deliberate labels to place on the subjects of their reports to attract attention. Of course, this can increase click rates, but it often lacks objectivity and fairness because the public's focus

> then concentrates on those labels without understanding what actually happened.

Interviewee V5 expressed frustration with the media's inclusion of unsolicited content, remarking,

> I told the media everything I could, but I found that the final report included some content that I never mentioned, which is the media's interpretation and speculation. I don't like this; I don't think others can interpret my story.

Interviewee V3 pointed out a fundamental failure in media reporting:

> They failed to do one thing, which is to help the public understand the nature of sexual violence. For instance, it's difficult to have evidence of sexual violence, and the plight faced by victims is different from other forms of violence. Public opinion tends to scrutinize the victim, so the media is responsible for educating the public, but they haven't done this. This is why I question the news media.

Meanwhile, interviewee V2 explained their preference for social media over traditional news outlets, saying,

> I chose social media as my first platform to speak out, not the news media because I feel that it allows me to explain my situation slowly and in detail. On the other hand, news media demand immediacy, which doesn't allow me to speak at my own pace and in detail.

These perspectives underline the critical need for media outlets to handle victim stories with more excellent care and ensure accuracy and sensitivity in their reporting practices. Victims value journalists who acknowledge their comfort levels upfront, permitting them to decline to answer questions that make them uncomfortable. This approach builds trust and empowers victims during the interview process. However, despite these efforts in initial interactions, victims often express dissatisfaction with how their stories are finally presented in the media. They point out issues such as sensationalism, where media outlets use provocative labels that distort public perception and focus on increasing viewership at the expense of accuracy and empathy.

Furthermore, victims are concerned about misinterpretations of their narratives, citing instances where their words were skewed or additional speculative content was included without their consent. This misrepresentation extends to a broader failure in media reporting, particularly around educating the public on the complexities of sexual violence, its evidentiary challenges, and the unique adversities faced by victims. This lack of depth in reporting can misdirect public scrutiny toward the victims instead of fostering a more informed and compassionate understanding. Given these challenges with traditional news media, some victims prefer sharing their experiences on social media, which allows for more detailed, personal, and controlled storytelling. This preference highlights the need for news media to adapt and reconsider their approaches to reporting victim stories, focusing more on ethical standards and the impactful role of media in shaping societal attitudes toward violence and trauma.

What Should the News Media Do to Provide Higher Quality Journalism?

This chapter evaluates the role of news media in Taiwan's #MeToo movement, highlighting its pivotal and insufficient aspects. While the Taiwanese media initially lagged in engaging with the #MeToo movement, the rise of social media has transformed how stories of sexual harassment are shared and discussed, with victims increasingly choosing online platforms over traditional media. Despite improved media sensitivity post-#MeToo, scholars argue that news outlets still need to fully utilize their gatekeeping function, often merely echoing social media rather than conducting thorough investigations. During the belated 2023 #MeToo movement, the news media and journalists aimed to provide more in-depth and thematic reporting, the effects of which were evident and impactful. However, to play a more important role, there is a need to enhance journalistic quality, requiring journalists to improve their skills and news outlets to allocate more resources and take greater social responsibilities. This chapter underscores the need for Taiwanese media to enhance its journalistic quality and commitment to balanced reporting to support social movements and contribute to systemic change effectively.

In the final chapters, I will address the suggestions for enhancing journalistic quality and outline strategic recommendations for media outlets better to fulfill their roles in societal transformation and accountability.

References

Andersen, N. B. (2017). Framing perfect victims: The February 2015 Copenhagen shooting in Danish newspapers. In Fonn BK, Hornmoen H, Hågvar YB, Hyde-Clarke N. *Putting a Face on It: Individual Exposure and Subjectivity in Journalism* (pp. 289–308). Cappelen Damm Akademisk, Oslo.

Blumell, L. E., & Huemmer, J. (2021). Reassessing balance: News coverage of Donald Trump's Access Hollywood scandal before and during# metoo. *Journalism, 22*(4), 937–955.

Chen, C. J., & Huang, C. L. (2023). Taiwan's belated #MeToo movement. *The Diplomat*. Retrieved from https://thediplomat.com/2023/07/taiwans-belated-metoo-movement/#:~:text=Over%20the%20past%20few%20weeks,analyzed%20%23MeToo%20in%20East%20Asia

Chen, H. R. (2023). The self-help MeToo Movement—The laziness of mainstream media in Taiwan. *Voicettank*. Retrieved from https://tw.news.yahoo.com/%E8%87%AA%E5%8A%9B%E6%95%91%E6%BF%9F%E7%9A%84metoo%E9%81%8B%E5%8B%95%E2%94%80%E2%94%80%E4%B8%BB%E6%B5%81%E5%AA%92%E9%AB%94%E6%80%A0%E6%83%B0%E7%9A%84%E5%8F%B0%E7%81%A3-230036710.html

Choi, Y. P. (2018). What kind of social movement is "#MeToo"? *MingPao*. Retrieved from https://www.mpweekly.com/culture/cu0001/metoo-%e4%bc%8a%e8%97%a4%e8%a9%a9%e7%b9%94-%e6%80%a7%e4%be%b5-86983

Coleman, R., McCombs, M., Shaw, D., & Weaver, D. (2009). Agenda setting. In *The handbook of journalism studies* (pp. 167–180). Routledge, London.

Feng, E. (2023). #MeToo in Taiwan: Over 100 public accusations of sexual violence in the last month. *NPR*. Retrieved from https://www.npr.org/2023/07/03/1185864055/-metoo-in-taiwan-over-100-public-accusations-of-sexual-violence-in-the-last-mont

Fuchs, C. (2014). Why Taiwanese are getting fed up with the island's salacious, in-your-face media. *Foreign Policy*.

Guo, L., & Vargo, C. (2015). The power of message networks: A big-data analysis of the network agenda setting model and issue ownership. *Mass Communication and Society*, *18*(5), 557–576.

Harrison, J. (2009). Gatekeeping and news selection as symbolic mediation. In Bob Franklin, Scott A. Eldridge II. *The Routledge companion to news and journalism* Edited By Bob Franklin, Scott A. Eldridge II (pp. 191–201). Routledge, London.

Leifermann, R. (2018). The framing of sexual harassment in German online newspapers: A critical discourse analysis of the online news coverage of the two biggest German newspapers on sexual harassment in the light of# MeToo in late 2017.

Majone, G. (2006). Agenda setting. In Michael Moran, Martin Rein, Robert E. Goodin. *The Oxford handbook of public policy* edited by Michael Moran, Martin Rein, Robert E. Goodin (pp. 228–250), New York.

McCombs, M. E., & Shaw, D. L. (1972). The agenda-setting function of mass media. *Public opinion quarterly*, *36*(2), 176–187.

Maxon, A. (2019). Majority of Taiwanese believe media doing a poor job. *Taipei Times*.

Mulupi, D., & Blumell, L. (2023). Gatekeeping rape culture: Kenyan news coverage of sexual abuse and femicide. *African Journalism Studies*, *44*(2), 153–170.

Peiser, W. (2000). Setting the journalist agenda: Influences from journalists' individual characteristics and from media factors. *Journalism & Mass Communication Quarterly*, *77*(2), 243–257.

Shoemaker, P. J., & Vos, T. (2009). *Gatekeeping theory*. Routledge, London.

Tsai, Y. W., & Su, H. (2016). Evolution of rape myths and sexual assaults in newspaper coverage. *Mass Communication Research*, *2016*(128), 85–134.

Wang, S. Y. (2021). Content and trend analysis of newspaper coverage of sexual harassment incidents in Taiwan. *Taiwan Journal of Sexology*, *27*(1), 23–49. https://doi.org/10.3966/160857872021052701002

5 Comparative Analysis of the News Media's Role in Tackling Sexual Violence in Mainland China, Hong Kong, and Taiwan

The role of news media in digital activism, particularly against sexual violence, is highly significant in shaping public narratives and mobilizing support. News outlets enhance the visibility of digital campaigns such as #MeToo by reporting on them, thus playing a critical role in elevating these movements from online hashtags to significant public discussions that can lead to real-world change (Bonilla & Rosa, 2015; Rodino-Colocino, 2014). While digital platforms provide innovative tools for activism, like blockchain technology used by Chinese students to bypass censorship (Zhai & Chen, 2018), mainstream news media still serve as a pivotal channel for broadening participant bases and influencing both public opinion and policy. The convergence of digital and traditional media not only helps sustain momentum for movements against sexual misconduct but also contests and redefines power dynamics within the sphere of activism, highlighting the intertwined roles of gender, race, and class in these processes (Clark, 2016; Keller et al., 2018). Despite the potential of digital media for surveillance and control (Chen & Xu, 2017) and the risks of polarization (Sunstein, 2012), the symbiotic relationship between digitally mediated activism and mainstream news coverage remains a foundational element in the fight against sexual violence, demonstrating the complex yet vital role of media in social change (Hilgartner & Bosk, 1988; Lee et al., 2017; McCarthy & Zaid, 1977; Risam, 2018). In this chapter, employing a gatekeeping theoretical framework, I scrutinize the setbacks, limitations, and other factors that may impede advancements in news media coverage. This analysis is instrumental in elucidating the underlying causes of observed declines in specific regions. I investigate the dynamics of media coverage concerning sexual violence in three distinct regions since the inception of the #MeToo movement in 2017. Specifically, this chapter identifies which regions have experienced a decrease and which have seen improvements in media coverage of sexual violence during the stated period.

Mainland China: Setbacks in News Media Coverage

In mainland China, the issue of sexual violence gained significant public attention in 2012, catalyzed by a younger generation of educated, tech-savvy

DOI: 10.4324/9781003474562-5

activists. This shift in awareness was particularly highlighted in June 2012 when a controversial advertisement by Shanghai Metro on Weibo suggested that women invited sexual harassment through their choice of clothing. The ad featured a woman in a sheer dress with visible underwear and a caption warning against "immodest" dressing due to the prevalence of "perverts." The campaign sparked widespread outrage and debate online over its victim-blaming message. In response, two women conducted a protest on the metro, covering their faces and wearing iron bowls over their chests to symbolize bras, holding signs stating, "I can be slutty, but you cannot harass me." This act of defiance and the vigorous online discussion it inspired brought significant attention to a growing coalition of young feminist activists. These activists, mainly college students and recent graduates from various professions, pushed for gender equality. They tackled issues like sexual violence, employment discrimination, and homophobia through creative protests, including performances like "Injured Bride" and "Occupy Men's Toilets" (Li & Li, 2017).

Despite the presence of active feminist groups and some traction within elite social media circles, the #MeToo movement has struggled to gain mainstream media coverage in China due to stringent state censorship. The government views the movement and its potential for forming transnational alliances with foreign human rights groups as threatening social stability and authority. As a result, while activists have attempted to use and adapt various hashtags like #WoYeShi and #Mitu (RiceBunny) to highlight issues of sexual misconduct, state censors have aggressively worked to suppress these discussions online. This dynamic underscores the complex challenges faced by movements like #MeToo in China, where government concerns over social order and the control of information clash with grassroots calls for change and social justice. Despite these hurdles, the persistence of young feminists and their innovative use of social media continues to challenge the status quo and keep the conversation about gender rights alive (Zeng, 2020).

I analyzed the portrayal of sexual harassment in news media from 2014 to 2018, as shown in Figure 5.1. The data reveal an increase in international coverage during 2017 and 2018, likely due to the influence of the #MeToo movement. During this time, Chinese state media capitalized on the heightened focus on sexual harassment, especially in the United States, to criticize Western culture and tout the moral superiority of socialist institutions. Between 2014 and 2016, coverage in mainland China primarily highlighted sexual harassment in the United States, India, and South Korea—this media strategy aimed to discredit political figures or movements opposed by the Chinese government. A notable instance was the December 2014 coverage of Chen Wei-ting from Taiwan's Sunflower Movement, who faced allegations of sexual misconduct. State media extensively reported on Chen, branding him a pro-independence figure and morally corrupt, using his case to undermine the movement he led. This narrative continued into 2018, with ongoing efforts to tarnish the reputation of Taiwan's democratic movements.

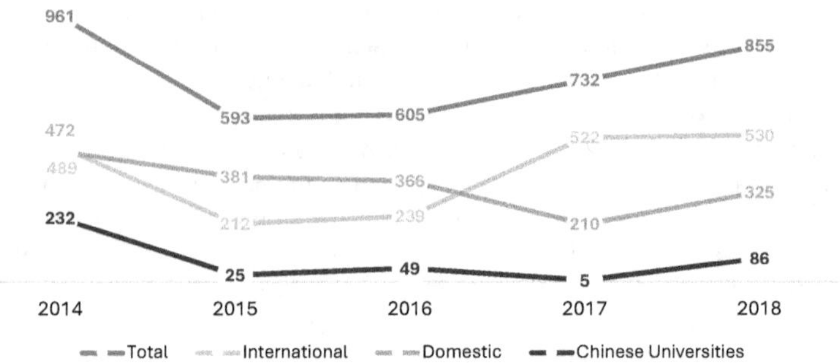

Figure 5.1 News Coverage of Sexual Harassment in *Mainland China Newspaper* (January 1, 2014–December 31, 2018).

Source: The first line represents the total number of news stories, the second shows the Domestic news stories, the third shows the international stories, and the final line shows the number of stories from Chinese Universities.

However, starting in January 2018, following the first major #MeToo case in China involving Dr. Luo Xixi, as discussed in earlier chapters, there was a noticeable shift in media coverage toward domestic incidents, particularly those involving universities. This case encouraged more victims to come forward and share their stories on social media, which quickly went viral. The surge in public attention allowed the news media more freedom to report on and facilitate public discussion on these issues, putting pressure on government bodies like the education department. Unfortunately, the coverage decreased sharply after students at Beijing University took collective offline action on campus, making #MeToo a sensitive issue and reducing media freedom on this topic.

A study on sexual harassment in higher education within mainland China underscores the challenges of digital activism under authoritarian rule, demonstrating how different stakeholders engage and influence each other in cases of sexual misconduct. Digital activism in China faces substantial external constraints, including state censorship, repression, coercion, and even the risk of arrest, which are hallmarks of authoritarian governance. Significant organizational challenges among individuals and within the media hinder collective action (Liao & Luqiu, 2022). In democratic societies, autonomous and professional NGOs play a crucial role in transforming online activism into effective policy engagement and public education. However, mainland China needs such independent organizations, leaving a gap that, ideally, the news media should fill. In democratic contexts, media often acts as a bridge, channeling grassroots activism into broader public discourse and policy influence. In mainland China, however, news media operate as extensions of the state apparatus and are heavily influenced by state policies and interests, limiting their capacity to support social movements independently.

The role of individuals within state institutions highlights another dynamic. While out-system activists can initiate digital campaigns, they lack the insider leverage necessary to effect policy changes. They often face increased repression risks, especially if perceived as collaborating with foreign entities. The repression of feminist groups and feminists in mainland China is one example. Conversely, insiders within state institutions can sometimes leverage their positions to effect change, as seen with open letters from 245 faculty at universities all over the country after the sexual harassment incident at Xiamen University in 2014. State news media reported this collective action, and then the Ministry of Education issued a code of conduct for teachers. Despite these constraints, the populace's desire for a fair and just society persists. However, for digital activism to be successful and drive social change, it must navigate the intricate power dynamics among various stakeholders and use sexual harassment in higher education in mainland China, including universities, the news media, policymakers, and advocates. After 2018, following the continuous crackdown on feminist groups, many influential feminists left China. Although they still attempt to exert influence from abroad, their impact is significantly limited. Moreover, the news media faces tightened control, with investigative journalists and investigative journalism virtually disappearing. As a result, high-quality journalism reporting on sexual violence has become increasingly rare.

In January 2022, a video on *Douyin (TikTok)* captured widespread attention: it depicted a middle-aged woman standing inside a doorless brick room, her expression of confusion. Despite the deep winter cold, she wore no coat. A metal chain around her neck tethered her to the wall. The video sparked widespread outrage and curiosity among social media users, who demanded answers to pressing questions: Who is she? Why was she chained? What were the circumstances under which she gave birth to eight children who lived with their father in the adjacent room? As public anger intensified, officials from Jiangsu Province, where the video was filmed, issued a brief statement. They identified the woman by the surname Yang and stated that she had been married to her husband since 1998, clarifying that she was not a victim of human trafficking. Diagnosed with a mental illness, the authorities assured, "She is currently receiving medical treatment and her family is being given additional support to ensure they spend a warm Spring Festival" (Wong, 2022).

Netizens gave her the moniker "Chain Woman," and her story ignited a movement reminiscent of #MeToo across Chinese social media. Many people came forward with harrowing tales of mothers, daughters, sisters, and classmates who had been kidnapped or disappeared. A resonant phrase circulated on social media: "We are not bystanders; we are merely survivors." On Weibo, the search term "Chain Woman" accumulated over ten billion views, drawing sympathy even from some of the government's most loyal supporters. This raised concerns that mishandling of the crisis could undermine governmental authority. Legal experts, academics, former journalists, and many bloggers educated the public on issues of human trafficking, forced marriages, and demographic challenges. They revisited literature and films about women trafficking, sparking deep reflections and discussions. Stories based on official news media reports and court documents particularly moved China's middle class: a Shanghai graduate student was kidnapped and sold during fieldwork but rescued after 71 days; a 13-year-old girl from Beijing was abducted on her way to school, sold to an abusive man, had a child at 15, and escaped at 19 (Yuan, 2022). However, the situation took a darker turn in February when two women attempting to visit the "Chain Woman" were detained and assaulted by local police. Their social media accounts and posts were swiftly deleted, and those who shared their stories received intimidating calls from the police. Authorities instructed bookstores to remove dedicated sections discussing the case, and professors were cautioned against discussing the matter with students.

In the wake of this incident, numerous online conspiracies emerged, speculating about the origins of the "Chain Woman" and challenging the official narrative amid widespread distrust of the government. Traditionally seen as the gatekeeper of accurate information, the news media failed to act in this capacity. Instead of correcting misinformation and fostering informed public discourse, the news media merely echoed official statements without investigating the myriad of online claims and theories. The news media's role was conspicuously passive, restricted to parroting official statements without delving into investigative journalism. This episode, which had the potential to reignite China's #MeToo movement, quickly faded from public view. This incident underscores the restricted role of the media in addressing sexual violence in mainland China. Limited to sporadic coverage of specific incidents, the news media cannot foster meaningful public discourse or provide comprehensive, accurate information. Consequently, this failure extends to the broader issue of protecting women's rights, leaving the public to rely on the internet for piecemeal and sometimes unreliable information before regulatory crackdowns suppress discussions.

Hong Kong: Concerns over Democratic Backsliding

To effectively assess the role of Hong Kong news media in addressing sexual violence, it is imperative to consider several pivotal factors that shape journalistic practices and their societal impact. Firstly, the constraints of media freedom due to the democratic backsliding in the region, thereby influencing how issues like sexual violence are reported. Secondly, the global challenges facing the news industry, economic pressures, and the quest for sensationalism can compromise the depth and quality of journalism. Understanding these factors is crucial as they directly affect the media's ability to engage with and influence public discourse and policy on sensitive issues such as sexual violence.

Democratic backsliding involves either the suspension of some or all of those fundamental constitutional rights that correspond to the basic rights or the exercise of those rights is obstructed without them being suspended (Wolkenstein, 2022). Rights-suspending democratic backsliding occurs when political actors temporarily deprive specific individuals or groups of fundamental constitutional rights to address urgent social or political issues. This approach is often justified by the necessity of extraordinary measures to resolve emergencies, an idea supported by existing legal frameworks that allow suspensions under specific, usually temporary conditions to restore normal constitutional operations once the crisis abates (Ferejohn & Pasquino, 2004). However, if these suspensions extend beyond their intended temporary scope or lead to an excessive concentration of power, they can constitute democratic backsliding, potentially resulting in more permanent authoritarian shifts (Huq & Ginsburg, 2018). This form of backsliding is particularly concerning as it frequently starts as a seemingly necessary response to an emergency but risks evolving into a more entrenched erosion of democratic norms. Rights-obstructing democratic backsliding refers to a gradual process where the ability of certain groups or individuals to exercise their constitutionally granted fundamental rights becomes increasingly difficult or impossible despite these rights not being formally suspended. This form of backsliding is characterized by the subtle and incremental introduction of new constitutional norms or laws that, while seemingly benign individually, collectively impede the effective exercise of fundamental rights. Kim Lane Scheppele (2013) emphasizes that the danger of these norms lies not in their individual effects but in their cumulative impact, which can significantly restrict rights when combined. This backsliding typically unfolds not through overt acts like a coup but through small, legal changes that gradually erode democratic practices and protections. This phenomenon is particularly insidious because it can occur under the guise of legitimate legal and constitutional reform. Consequently, what might initially appear as reasonable adjustments to the constitutional order can lead to significant restrictions on rights, either as an unintended consequence of poor constitutional design or as a part of a deliberate strategy to alter the nature of the state more permanently. Thus, rights-obstructing democratic backsliding represents a subtle yet profound threat to democracy as it systematically undermines the practical availability of rights ostensibly protected by law.

The analysis of press freedom in Hong Kong under the National Security Law (NSL) reveals a strategic use of legal frameworks to control the media, signifying a shift toward authoritarian practices masked as national security measures. The Hong Kong government utilizes these laws to significantly curtail press freedom, justifying such actions as necessary to maintain public order and protect against threats to the city's stability. This justification is typical of authoritarian regimes seeking to maintain a semblance of legality and legitimacy while suppressing dissent and controlling the media narrative. The impact on journalism since the enactment of the NSL has been profound. Prominent pro-democracy newspapers like *Apple Daily* and online platforms like Stand News were forced to shut down following arrests and financial pressures from legal actions under the NSL. This direct assault on media entities critical of the government is a clear indication of the law's use as a tool for political suppression.

Moreover, anticipating legal repercussions has led journalists and media outlets to self-censorship. The fear of potential legal consequences has resulted in a significant reduction in critical or investigative reporting on sensitive issues, particularly those that might be perceived as opposing the government or the policies of the Chinese mainland. The decline of investigative journalism, influenced by political and economic constraints, has notably affected the quality of reporting on complex issues like sexual violence. With thorough investigations, newspapers can avoid merely scratching the surface of incidents without exposing underlying causes or holding powerful entities accountable. This evolving landscape has seen Hong Kong's ranking in the Reporters without Borders' press freedom index plummet from 80 in 2020 to 148 in 2022, illustrating the region's rapid decline of journalistic freedom. The situation in Hong Kong represents a rights-obstructing form of democratic backsliding, where the government selectively uses legal tools to block the exercise of journalistic freedoms. Unlike a complete suspension of rights, which would imply an overt removal of all freedoms, this approach involves obstructing rights through legal means, enabling the government to maintain an appearance of legality and order while effectively silencing dissent and controlling the media landscape. This subtle yet systematic approach to legalizing press control underscores a calculated move toward authoritarianism under the guise of legal and social stability (Lee & Chan, 2023).

The analysis of news media reporting on sexual harassment in orientation camps in Hong Kong during 2023 and 2024 highlights a failure in media oversight to effectively probe and address the structural issues that necessitate government action to enhance existing mechanisms. This includes legal frameworks, where there is a need to amend laws to mirror societal changes, and law enforcement practices, which require improvements to motivate more victims to report incidents. Moreover, significant deficiencies in the educational structure are evident, as revealed by the EOC's 2022 data on sex education in Hong Kong's middle schools (EOC, 2022). The data points to insufficient class hours, with 13.8% of schools not offering sex education in the 2018/2019 academic year and nearly half providing minimal instructional time. Additionally, curriculum content often overlooks critical topics such as sexual orientation and gender equality, and a substantial number of educators lack professional development in sex education. These issues underscore the urgent need for the government to implement comprehensive sex education starting earlier, possibly in primary schools, to enhance gender awareness and establish a foundational basis for preventing sexual crimes, thereby addressing the root causes of sexual harassment and enhancing student safety and education overall. The decline of investigative journalism, influenced by political and economic constraints, has also notably affected the quality of reporting on complex issues like sexual violence. Without thorough investigations, newspapers risk merely scratching the surface of incidents without exposing underlying causes or holding powerful entities accountable.

Some might argue that since the implementation of the NSL, the Hong Kong government has been proactively addressing issues such as sexual violence. For instance, the EOC conducted surveys to address sexual harassment issues. However, a closer examination of the government's narrative on solving sexual harassment in O'Camps reveals that the lawmakers, who are loyal to Beijing or are patriotic, along with senior government officials, are primarily focused on one objective: stripping students and universities of their autonomy. The head of the EOC explicitly stated that they do not have the authority to mandate universities to implement measures. They can only offer suggestions, yet lawmakers appear dissatisfied, seeking greater government control over campuses. The targeting of universities, especially students, sends a message to the public that these young people need to be re-educated as they could otherwise negatively influence society. They exaggerate individual cases to convince the public that orientation camps are morally corrupt and should be abolished. Student societies, significant in Hong Kong activism, are now dwindling amid a broader crackdown on dissent (Chan, 2022). As student unions are forcibly disbanded or dissolved due to dwindling student participation, orientation camps, traditionally considered non-political, are increasingly seen as potential platforms for mobilizing and organizing students. This trend of tightening control raises concerns about the future of autonomy: if student autonomy is withdrawn, can university autonomy still be sustained?

The government and politicians' voices are broadcast through the media to the public domain, where the news media report but do not question whether this approach is optimal. This differs from past practices where policies or administrative measures were introduced following public discussions, allowing diverse voices to be heard. The only critical piece, published by Ming Pao on October 11, 2023, by columnist Allen Tien, questions the harsh rhetoric in the legislature that does not reflect the truth but serves as a pretext to regulate student activities. Tian notes,

> The recent measures by universities to increasingly regulate student activities, such as not recognizing student unions, reclaiming their premises, and not assisting with fee collection, often managed by university student affairs offices instead of student-led associations, suggest that the orientation camp incidents are merely excuses to tighten control.
>
> (Tien, 2023)

In Hong Kong, news media coverage of sexual violence often perpetuates rape culture, reinforcing harmful myths and stereotypes. This issue is highlighted in studies by Leung (2019) and Hernández (2018), which focused on intimate partner violence (IPV). Leung's analysis of local newspapers like *Apple Daily* and Ming Pao reveals that reporting frequently blames victims, stereotypes abusers, and neglects women's rights, thereby perpetuating unequal power dynamics and reinforcing gender stereotypes. Hernández finds that while most reports justify perpetrators' actions and treat IPV incidents as isolated crimes, some recognize the cultural underpinnings of women's subordination under Confucian values. Together, these findings indicate that Hong Kong's news media contributes to marginalizing IPV survivors and obscuring the systemic nature of this violence.

The emergence of the #MeToo movement in Hong Kong has remained relatively the same narrative. Examining two news media outlets' online #MeToo stories illustrates this variability. Two news media organizations have adopted a specific approach to reporting sexual harassment by tagging related news articles with the #MeToo label. This strategy facilitates readers in quickly finding and tracking these issues, reflecting the influence of the #MeToo movement in raising public awareness about sexual harassment. Moreover, the use of these tags highlights the varying attitudes and focuses of the media when addressing reports on sexual harassment.HK01's #MeToo stories focus on celebrity sex scandals, often presented sensationalistically, serving as a gateway to lurid content rather than a platform for serious discussion (HK01).

In contrast, the Hong Kong Economic Journal's #MeToo stories, from November 30, 2017, to May 31, 2024, featured 167 reports. Initially, it echoed the global #MeToo movement with a focus on the local case of Vera Liu. However, starting May 4, 2018, the subsequent reporting shifted to international celebrities and public figures, suggesting a detachment from local issues (hket). This variability in reporting underlines the continued existence of rape culture within Hong Kong's news media, even in the wake of global movements aimed at addressing these very issues.

Taiwan: Failed as the Primary Advocate

Among the three Chinese language-speaking societies, Taiwan stands out as the only liberal democracy where the media enjoys full freedom, and citizens benefit from unrestricted freedom of speech. According to Reporters Without Borders, in 2024, Taiwan ranks 27th out of 180 countries, while Hong Kong is positioned at 135 and mainland China at 172. Reporters Sans Frontières (RSF) notes that Taiwan, officially the Republic of China and the world's 21st largest economy, broadly respects the principles of media freedom, serving as a role model of press freedom in the Asia-Pacific region. Despite this, Taiwanese journalists contend with a highly polarized media environment dominated by sensationalism and the pursuit of profit. The Taiwanese public has one of the lowest levels of trust in media among democracies, with a trust rate of only 28%, according to a Reuters Institute survey in 2022, placing last in the

Asia-Pacific region. This issue is compounded by widespread sensationalism, the pursuit of profit over journalistic integrity, and the influence of business and political interests in media ownership, which can lead to conflicts of interest and undermine the credibility of news reporting. Additionally, the rapid transition from a controlled to a free press has led to a chaotic media environment with varying quality, further eroding trust. These challenges are exacerbated by inadequate regulatory oversight and a general lack of media literacy among the public, making it difficult for consumers to evaluate the reliability of news sources critically (Tse, 2024).

If we look at ranking, Taiwan has also performed excellent on gender equality. According to the Gender Inequality Index (GII) published by the United Nations Development Programme (UNDP), which measures the development of gender inequality in countries worldwide by analyzing five indicators across three dimensions—reproductive health, empowerment, and the labor market—Taiwan ranks 7th out of 171 countries and 1st in Asia in 2024. In 2019, Taiwan became the first country in Asia to legalize same-sex marriage. In Taiwan, a subgroup of socially progressive legislators, NGOs, and other stakeholders have implemented laws and institutional mechanisms aimed at promoting gender equality and combating various forms of discrimination. Nonetheless, these values have not yet permeated the social mainstream. While parts of Taiwanese society have embraced diverse sexual identities and orientations, ongoing debates about sexual harassment reveal that traditional gender equality issues between men and women are still deeply influenced by patriarchal attitudes. A 2022 survey by the Ministry of Labor found that 3.3% of female employees and 1.3% of male workers had experienced sexual harassment at work. However, the ministry overseeing Taiwan's population of 23.3 million received only 165 complaints that year.

Compared to mainland China, where the news media cannot openly discuss the #MeToo movement yet where discussions still flourish on social media, Taiwan only began a similar earnest debate in 2023. This debate, initially sparked by allegations of sexual violence within the Democratic People's Party (DPP), raised concerns about the potential exploitation of the issue for partisan gains in the upcoming presidential elections. However, the conversation quickly expanded beyond political circles to encompass the entertainment, sports, and education sectors. This broadened dialogue across various societal sectors hinted at the potential for deeper and more enduring change (McCombs & Valenzuela, 2020). The news media played a pivotal role in this transition, showcasing improved journalistic quality and illustrating how press freedom can shape public discussions.

Despite these positive beginnings, the momentum was short-lived as the news media focused on celebrities. This evolution, from a media phenomenon centered around celebrities' lives to a more reflective discourse on everyday instances of gender-related power inequalities and sexual violence, failed to materialize. Instead, the celebrity-centric reporting detracted from the quality of public discourse (Linkof, 2020). By focusing on celebrities, the news media skewed public perception and overshadowed more pressing societal issues, placing undue emphasis on individual personalities rather than systemic problems. Such coverage, often superficial and sensationalist, appeals more to entertainment values than to civic engagement or educational objectives. This type of journalism frequently fails to challenge the audience to think critically or engage deeply with the underlying issues, thus limiting the potential for meaningful societal progress. Initially a force for significant discourse, the news media ultimately diminished its impact by prioritizing celebrity narratives over substantive, issue-based journalism (Arbaoui et al., 2020).

The #MeToo debate in Western countries has revolutionized the way gender issues are discussed in everyday settings, paving the way for in-depth public discourse that extends beyond mere surface-level conversations. Even in mainland China, where the market dynamics have begun to leverage feminism as a marketing tool despite inherent challenges, there has been a noticeable increase in gender awareness. Similarly, Taiwan has seen a burgeoning debate aimed at addressing everyday life issues through comprehensive social discussions. At the peak of the #MeToo movement's visibility, the news media played a crucial role not just in reporting cases but in educating the public about what constitutes sexual harassment. For example, the common term "eating tofu" was explained in detail, educating the public that actions described by this phrase actually constitute sexual harassment, a clarification prompted by academic insights (Chen, 2023a). Subsequent media follow-ups, such as the *China Times*' publication of a list of the top ten sexual harassment behaviors (2023), underscored the role of the media in shaping public understanding and response to these issues. In addition to tracking individual cases, some media outlets pursued deeper investigative journalism to examine systemic issues. *Mirror Weekly*, for instance, ran a series on the challenges associated with implementing laws related to gender equality and sexual harassment (Chiang & Chien, 2023). *The Reporter* organized online data revealing that despite the presence of laws like the Gender Equality Education Act, the Gender Equality in Employment Act, and the Sexual Harassment Prevention Act, the average fine for offenders over the past two decades stood at merely NT$18,000. Furthermore, although approximately 200,000 people experience sexual harassment at work annually, only 20% choose to file complaints. It provides serious reporting to explore the structure problems, especially in the legal system (The Reporter, 2023).

These feature series highlighted individual violations and initiated a broader discussion on why these protective laws are underutilized and whether the issues lie within the laws themselves or the societal attitudes toward them. Such in-depth reporting facilitates better public discussions by allowing the audience to understand the systemic roots of gender-related issues rather than just reacting to individual incidents (Bachmann et al., 2022). This approach empowers the public to think critically about the effectiveness of existing legal frameworks and the broader societal changes necessary to combat gender inequality and sexual harassment effectively.

Despite Taiwan's comprehensive laws, the amendment of these laws coincided with the onset of election coverage, causing the #MeToo movement to lose significant media attention. As a result, the depth and frequency of news reporting on #MeToo declined, leading public discussion to devolve back to isolated incidents quickly. The majority of media outlets continue to engage in "horse-race" style reporting; this approach allows the narratives of victims or whistleblowers to be dismissed as merely "one side of the story" once the accused turn the matter over to the judiciary, invite lawsuits, or decline to comment. News media must implement a stringent gatekeeping system and uphold professional verification standards. Through investigative and feature reports that present diverse testimonies and build a comprehensive narrative, the responses of "no comment" and "welcome to sue" can be rendered ineffective and unavoidable. This method ensures that the testimonies of victims of sexual harassment and assault are given proper weight and integrated as a real part of societal discourse—a level of media treatment and protection that many accusers in Taiwan currently lack (Chen, 2023b).

However, the focus in Taiwan often remains disproportionately on the victims themselves, scrutinizing their actions and questioning their credibility. This scrutiny can lead to a climate of suspicion, where victims face tough questioning and, in some cases, are subjected to intimidation via legal threats or public shaming. This situation underscores a significant failure in the media's role as a gatekeeper. Instead of fostering a nuanced and ongoing discussion that could lead to societal change, the media often fails to set a robust agenda that maintains the public's focus on the systemic issues at play.

In contrast to regions like Hong Kong and mainland China, where the discourse might offer somewhat different dynamics, victims in Taiwan seem to endure even harsher examinations, and the accused often find it easier to dodge full accountability. Particularly concerning is the leniency with which male perpetrators are treated in public debates. There is a noticeable lack of pressure on men to introspect and critically assess their own behaviors and attitudes toward women. This reflects a broader societal issue where meaningful change remains elusive without sustained media attention and in-depth reporting that challenges the public to think critically. The media must embrace its responsibility to rigorously examine these issues, ensuring that all parties are held accountable and that the dialogue moves beyond individual incidents to address the root causes of sexual harassment and gender inequality.

Despite Taiwan enjoying a high level of press freedom, which starkly contrasts with the state-controlled media environment in mainland China, Taiwanese media still struggles to facilitate public discussions aimed at social change effectively. In Hong Kong, recent changes in the media environment have similarly constrained the impact of news media in social movements. However, the case of Taiwan highlights the crucial role of quality journalism.

Unlike in regions where media may be under tight government scrutiny or subject to political pressures, Taiwan's relatively free press has the potential to contribute significantly to social movements like #MeToo. This underscores the importance of maintaining journalistic integrity and dedication to in-depth reporting that informs, challenges, and engages society. By doing so, the media can play a transformative role, turning public discourse into a powerful catalyst for social change.

References

Arbaoui, B., De Swert, K., & Van der Brug, W. (2020). Sensationalism in news coverage: A comparative study in 14 television systems. *Communication Research*, *47*(2), 299–320.

Bachmann, P., Eisenegger, M., & Ingenhoff, D. (2022). Defining and measuring news media quality: Comparing the content perspective and the audience perspective. *The International Journal of Press/Politics*, *27*(1), 9–37.

Bonilla, Y., & Rosa, J. (2015). #Ferguson: Digital protest, hashtag ethnography, and the racial politics of social media in the United States. *American Ethnologist*, *42*(1), 4–17.

Chan, T. (2022). The death of Hong Kong's university student union. *The Diplomat.* Retrieved from https://thediplomat.com/2022/04/the-death-of-hong-kongs-university-student-unions/

Chen, H. R. (2023b). Self-help #MeToo Movement: The laziness of mainstream media in Taiwan. *Voicettank.* Retrieved from https://voicettank.org/%E8%87%AA%E5%8A%9B%E6%95%91%E6%BF%9F%E7%9A%84metoo%E9%81%8B%E5%8B%95%E4%B8%BB%E6%B5%81%E5%AA%92%E9%AB%94%E6%80%A0%E6%83%B0%E7%9A%84%E5%8F%B0%E7%81%A3/

Chen, J., & Xu, Y. (2017). Why do authoritarian regimes allow citizens to voice opinions publicly? *The Journal of Politics*, *79*(3), 792–803.

Chen, M. H. (2023a). Why has the MeToo movement only emerged in Taiwan now? Have any of the accused truly faced social ostracization? *The News Lens*. Retrieved from https://www.thenewslens.com/article/187661

Chiang, I. T., & Chien, C. S (2023). Unsquashable rose: When the law becomes a weapon for suspects of sexual violence. *Mirror Media*. Retrieved from https://www.mirrormedia.mg/story/20230724pol001

China Times. (2023). Top 10 common tactics of sexual harassment! Turns out you've been groped too. *China Times*. Retrieved from https://www.chinatimes.com/realtimenews/20230612001063-260405?chdtv

Clark, R. (2016). "Hope in a hashtag": The discursive activism of #WhyIStayed. *Feminist Media Studies*, *16*(5), 788–804.

EOC. (2022). EOC releases findings of a study on comprehensive sexuality education in secondary schools of Hong Kong. *Equal Opportunity Committee*. Retrieved from https://www.eoc.org.hk/en/PressRelease/Detail/18517

Ferejohn, J., & Pasquino, P. (2004). The law of the exception: A typology of emergency powers. *International Journal of Constitutional Law*, *2*(2), p.210–239.

Hernández, M. (2018). "Killed out of love": A frame analysis of domestic violence coverage in Hong Kong. *Violence against Women*, *24*(12), 1454–1473.

Hilgartner, S., & Bosk, C. L. (1988). The rise and fall of social problems: A public arenas model. *American journal of Sociology*, *94*(1), 53–78.

HK01. #MeToo. *HK01*. Retrieved from https://www.hk01.com/tag/28805

Hket. #MeToo. *Hong Kong Economic Times*. Retrieved from https://service.hket.com/search/result?dis=contenttagid&keyword=2658

Huq, A., & Ginsburg, T. (2018). How to lose a constitutional democracy. *UCLA L. Rev.*, *65*, 78.

Keller, J., Mendes, K., & Ringrose, J. (2018). Speaking "unspeakable things:" Documenting digital feminist responses to rape culture. *Journal of Gender Studies*, *27*(1), 22–36.

Lee, F. L., & Chan, C. K. (2023). Legalization of press control under democratic backsliding: The case of post-national security law Hong Kong. *Media, Culture & Society*, *45*(5), 916–931.

Lee, F. L., Chen, H. T., & Chan, M. (2017). Social media use and university students' participation in a large-scale protest campaign: The case of Hong Kong's Umbrella Movement. *Telematics and Informatics*, *34*(2), 457–469.

Leung, L. C. (2019). Deconstructing the myths about intimate partner violence: A critical discourse analysis of news reporting in Hong Kong. *Journal of Interpersonal Violence*, *34*(11), 2227–2245.

Li, J., & Li, X. (2017). Media as a core political resource: The young feminist movements in China. *Chinese Journal of Communication*, *10*(1), 54–71.

Liao, S., & Luqiu, L. R. (2022). # MeToo in China: The dynamic of digital activism against sexual assault and harassment in higher education. *Signs: Journal of women in culture and society*, *47*(3), 741–764.

Linkof, R. (2020). *Public images: Celebrity, photojournalism, and the making of the tabloid press*. Routledge.

McCarthy, J. D., & Zaid, M. N. (1977). Resource mobilization and social movements: A partial theory. *American Journal of Sociology*, *82*(6), 1212–1241.

McCombs, M., & Valenzuela, S. (2020). *Setting the agenda: Mass media and public opinion*. John Wiley & Sons, Cambridge.

The Reporter. (2023). The delayed #MeToo Movement in Taiwan: How to move forward after uncovering the scars? *The Reporter*. Retrieved from https://www.twreporter.org/topics/taiwan-me-too

Risam, R. (2018). Now you see them: Self-representation and the refugee selfie. *Popular Communication*, *16*(1), 58–71.

Rodino-Colocino, M. (2014). #YesAllWomen: Intersectional mobilization against sexual assault is radical (again). *Feminist Media Studies*, *14*(6), 1113–1115.

Scheppele, K. L. (2013). The rule of law and the frankenstate: Why governance checklists do not work. *Governance*, *26*(4), 559–562.

Sunstein, C. (2012). The daily we: Is the Internet really a blessing for democracy? *Reagle.org*. Retrieved from https://reagle.org/joseph/2003/12/sunstein-daily-we-boston-review.html

Tien, A. (2023). Excessive regulation of student activities is detrimental to society. *Ming Pao*. Retrieved from https://news.mingpao.com/pns/%E8%A7%80%E9%BB%9E/article/20231011/s00012/1696957141567/%E7%94%B0%E6%96%B9%E6%BE%A4-%E9%81%8E%E5%BA%A6%E8%A6%8F%E7%AE%A1%E5%AD%B8%E7%94%9F%E6%B4%BB%E5%8B%95-%E5%B0%8D%E7%A4%BE%E6%9C%83%E7%84%A1%E7%9B%8A

Tse, C. H. (2024). Alternative news values in community citizen journalism: The case of PeoPo in Taiwan. *Journalism Practice*, 1–18. https://www.tandfonline.com/doi/full/10.1080/17512786.2024.2385999

Wolkenstein, F. (2022). What is democratic backsliding. *Constellations*, *30*(3), 261–275.

Wong, J. (2022). Video of mentally ill woman chained in shack stirs anger in China. *The New York Times*. Retrieved from https://cn.nytimes.com/china/20220204/china-chained-woman-video/dual/

Yuan, L. (2022). Seeking truth and justice, Chinese see themselves in a chained woman. *The New York Times*. Retrieved from https://www.nytimes.com/2022/03/01/business/china-chained-woman-social-media.html

Zeng, J. (2020). # MeToo as connective action: A study of the anti-sexual violence and anti-sexual harassment campaign on Chinese social media in 2018. *Journalism Practice*, *14*(2), 171–190.

Zhai, K., & Chen, L. Y. (2018). Chinese #MeToo student activists use blockchain to fight censors. *Bloomberg*. Retrieved from https://www.bloomberg.com/news/articles/2018-04-24/chinese-metoo-student-activists-use-blockchain-to-fight-censors

6 Confronting the Frontlines

Challenges and Innovations in Journalism Covering Sexual Violence

In August 2011, as a television reporter, I hosted a news feature segment. One day, I came across a post on Weibo from a female college student who had experienced sexual harassment in the workplace. She reported the incident to the police, but they declined to take her case, leaving her with no choice but to seek media attention. I spent some time convincing the show's producer of the importance of covering this issue, arguing that workplace sexual harassment concerns the public interest. I understood the editor's reluctance; topics like these do not attract high viewership, and he felt it was too minor issue to dedicate an hour-long program. Eventually, I got the green light. The immediate challenge was finding more cases to report on, as relying solely on one person's account made it difficult to verify details through cross-examination. Finally, five women agreed to be interviewed, along with the lawyer who accompanied them to the police station. The program was successfully aired.

However, the episode received little response and had low viewership ratings. Other news media showed little interest in the topic of workplace sexual harassment, although it is a persistent issue. During my tenure at the media company, three incidents occurred in our offices in the United States, Hong Kong, and Beijing, exposing me to different approaches under varying legal and cultural environments. In the United States, a colleague handed over recordings to the American news media and gave interviews when the company failed to respond internally, which forced the company to address the issue legally. In Hong Kong, a colleague went directly to the police, leading to officers taking the accused supervisor away. Although there was no prosecution, it was widely discussed. In Beijing, the matter was ignored. In 2017, a survey among female journalists in China revealed that over 80% of 255 participants had experienced sexual harassment. This culture within Chinese news media tends to inadvertently and deliberately overlook the issue of workplace sexual harassment (Lai, 2018).

However, the persistent and unwavering focus of the news media on issues of sexual violence is essential for driving change. Also in 2011, I worked on a feature about domestic violence legislation. This topic came into the spotlight due to a high-profile domestic violence case involving Li Yang, founder of Crazy English, whom his American wife accused on social media (Zhang

DOI: 10.4324/9781003474562-6

& Guo, 2011). Due to Li Yang's fame, the case quickly became one of the hottest topics on social media, attracting extensive media coverage. Scholars and nonprofit organizations advocating for domestic violence legislation in China seized the public's interest and attention to push for media advocacy on legislation. However, the news media response was limited, largely overshadowed by the sensational nature of celebrity domestic violence cases. When I decided to cover this topic, I chose to interview ordinary people and those who had been advocating for legislation for over a decade, including scholars, lawyers, and nonprofits, focusing on the urgency of legislation. I had to convince my colleagues not to pursue interviews with Li Yang and his wife, knowing that it would attract viewers but detract from the focus on legislative issues. Ultimately, I opted to feature victims of various ages and socioeconomic backgrounds to highlight the universality of the problem. The law was finally implemented in 2016 as a response to public concern by policymakers to protect women's rights. That was the golden age of journalism; news media constantly acted as the factor to facilitate public discussion and push policy changes. China's one-child policy reform illustrates how news media, scholars, and non-governmental organizations (NGOs) can collaboratively influence policy changes. This multifaceted cooperation highlighted the power of collective advocacy and information dissemination in shaping public policy.

To improve the coverage of sexual violence in news reporting, whether in terms of increasing attention or enhancing the quality of reports, there is room for improvement within news media organizations themselves, regardless of external factors like the degree of media control or the prevalence of misogyny in the culture. The news media can and should do better.

One of the main reasons I can address issues related to sexual violence is that I am not only a journalist and a host but also the director of the news department. This means I can set the agenda and make decisions, insisting that commercial interests must yield to the public good. My focus on these issues stems from being a woman who regularly encounters sexual harassment in the workplace, such as having to listen to inappropriate jokes at dinner tables and experiencing unwelcome physical advances from interviewees during field reports. However, most journalists lack sufficient resources and the support of their superiors to negotiate these issues effectively. If editors lack adequate awareness of gender issues or if they have other concerns, such as the fear of reporting on sexual violence—especially online harassment allegations—which could potentially lead to legal actions, it becomes crucial to have a newsroom that is conscious of gender dynamics.

Newsroom Culture

The culture within newsrooms, along with a consciousness about gender and diversity, is crucial in shaping the news that reaches the public. Research by Steiner (2019) emphasizes how historical biases have often resulted in female journalists being pigeonholed by their gender identity, influencing both the expectations placed upon them and the evaluation of their professional capabilities. This recognition of biased treatment underscores the urgent need to foster a newsroom culture that actively challenges these stereotypes and strives for gender equity. Similarly, findings by Kim and Yoon (2009) demonstrate that female reporters in South Korea tend to provide more balanced and stereotype-free coverage when reporting on female Cabinet members, suggesting that gender diversity in newsrooms leads to more nuanced reporting. Trussardi (2021) further highlights the significant role of gender perspectives in journalism, advocating for a newsroom culture that recognizes and utilizes gender as a critical category to foster more inclusive and socially conscious journalistic practices. Together, these studies emphasize the need for culturally sensitive, diverse, and gender-conscious newsrooms, which directly affect the quality and societal impact of news reporting.

The need for cultural transformation within newsrooms across mainland China, Hong Kong, and Taiwan is underscored by the problematic coverage of sexual violence, as exemplified by mainstream U.S. media's handling of the #MeToo movement. Cuklanz (2020) critiques the U.S. news coverage, highlighting a persistent perpetrator-centric narrative that sidelines victims' experiences reminiscent of earlier flawed reporting practices on rape and sexual assault. Despite this, there are glimpses of progress in the United States, where some reports acknowledge the roles of corporate and rape cultures in abuses of power. In contrast, newsrooms in Chinese-speaking societies face unique challenges: mainland China operates under stringent government control, gradually influencing Hong Kong's media landscape toward a similar restrictive environment. At the same time, Taiwan maintains a relatively open media system. Nonetheless, all three regions have significant room for improvement in fostering a newsroom culture that prioritizes gender issues and combats sexual violence more effectively. This is further supported by Heckman's (2023) study, which, through interviews with U.S. gender-beat journalists, reveals an evolving recognition of the importance of dedicated coverage to issues of gender, race, sexuality, class, and geography. This reflection on the U.S. context serves as a model approach for Chinese-language newsrooms, highlighting the necessity to overhaul traditional practices and allocate adequate resources toward comprehensive and empathetic gender reporting, aiming for a cultural shift that transcends mere compliance and ingrains more profound societal changes.

The suggested transformations for newsrooms in Hong Kong, Taiwan, and mainland China focus on several key areas to foster a more inclusive and responsive environment. Firstly, the relationship between editors and reporters must evolve, promoting the democratization of the newsroom where reporters' pitches are met with positive responses rather than judged based solely on editors' personal experiences and values. This shift would encourage a broader range of stories and perspectives. Several reporters have mentioned that when pitching stories on sexual harassment, they often face considerable challenges. Completing such reports can be time-consuming, and supervisors are typically reluctant to allocate the necessary resources. This change in the newsroom dynamic is essential to foster diverse and in-depth reporting.

Additionally, although women journalists make up a significant portion of the workforce in these regions, management remains predominantly male. Addressing and changing the biases against female journalists in the newsroom is crucial for achieving true gender equality. Achieving this equality is fundamental not only for fairness but also for providing better coverage of gender issues, including sexual violence. This ensures that the reporting is more comprehensive, empathetic, and informed, reflecting the nuances and complexities of such sensitive topics. Moreover, tackling sexual harassment within the newsroom itself is equally important. Creating a safe and supportive environment for all staff will enhance journalism's quality and integrity.

The third significant recommendation for enhancing journalistic practice entails a shift from episodic reporting to a more comprehensive series that scrutinizes systemic issues underlying individual cases. This form of journalism captivates readers and enriches the narrative style, rendering stories more compelling and informative. The transition to in-depth reporting necessitates extensive modifications in newsroom operations. Critical to this process is the allocation of increased time and budget dedicated to rigorous research and complex storytelling. Further, it is imperative to augment training programs in investigative journalism and multimedia storytelling, supported by editorial guidance from specialists adept in long-form journalism. Collaborative endeavors with external organizations and integrating sophisticated data analysis and digital publishing tools are essential. Actively engaging the audience through regular solicitation of feedback and assessing the impact of reports effectively refine content. Additionally, cultivating a newsroom culture that prioritizes meticulous reporting over rapid output and acknowledging the efforts of journalists engaged in long-form projects are vital for fostering depth and enhancing the quality of journalistic output. Together, these concerted efforts will empower newsrooms to produce insightful series that probe into systemic issues, broadening public understanding and significantly enriching the landscape of journalism.

The fourth suggestion to enhance journalistic practice involves establishing a dedicated beat for gender issues reporting, which is crucial given the evolving complexity and importance of gender-related topics in society. This specialized focus allows journalists to cultivate substantial knowledge and nuanced understanding by continuously covering these topics. Allocating experienced journalists or training enthusiastic reporters interested in gender issues; building robust networks with advocacy groups, academic experts, community leaders, and policymakers; and maintaining continual coverage are strategic actions crucial for in-depth reporting. This constant attention helps identify emerging trends, track ongoing developments, and provide timely updates. With specialized knowledge and well-established networks, these journalists can explore more profound systemic inequalities, intersectionality, and the impacts of policy changes, thus producing high-quality reports. Newsrooms should also provide ongoing education in gender studies and related fields, engage with audiences through various platforms to foster dialogue, and regularly assess the impact of their reporting on public discourse and policy changes. This comprehensive approach enhances journalism's quality and ensures responsible, informed reporting that contributes positively to societal understanding and change.

Lastly, conducting regular reviews of gender representation within the newsroom, in terms of staffing and content, is essential to ensure ongoing progress toward achieving gender balance and sensitivity. This involves systematically evaluating the roles and contributions of staff across different genders and scrutinizing how gender issues are represented and addressed in the content produced. Such reviews help identify potential biases or gaps in coverage and staffing, fostering a more inclusive workplace and content that reflects diverse perspectives. Implementing these reviews as a routine practice can drive continuous improvement and awareness around gender issues within journalistic operations. Importantly, even in non-democratic societies where press freedoms can be constrained, fostering a culture change within newsrooms can provide journalists and editors who remain committed to the principles of journalism with increased latitude to operate. These strategies, particularly pivotal for newsrooms in Taiwan, are instrumental in propelling the media landscape toward a more inclusive, democratic, and ethically robust framework. By embracing these practices, newsrooms can play a crucial role in shaping a more informed and equitable society, enhancing the quality of journalism and ensuring it contributes positively to the public discourse on gender and beyond. This cultural shift within newsrooms allows committed journalists and editors to enjoy more room to maneuver, promoting more robust and impactful journalism even in challenging environments.

Institutionalize Support for Journalists

Institutionalizing support for journalists is critical not just in the realm of general reporting, but it becomes especially pivotal when addressing sensitive issues like sexual violence. This multifaceted support, encompassing practical, legal, and mental health aspects, enables journalists to perform their duties effectively and ethically across all topics. Providing resources such as access to specialized databases, contact networks, and advanced technology ensures that journalists can conduct in-depth research and produce high-quality reporting on any subject, including the intricacies of sexual violence. It is essential to offer robust protection and legal advice, particularly when handling sensitive issues, safeguarding journalists against litigation, and ensuring their freedom to report the truth. Additionally, the intense nature of covering topics like sexual violence necessitates strong mental health support through counseling and support programs to help journalists cope with the stresses and emotional toll of their work. These supports are not only necessary for maintaining the integrity and vitality of journalism but also for ensuring that journalists can continue to shed light on critical issues like sexual violence, contributing to a more informed and just society.

Code of Ethics

A code of ethics is critical for journalists as it ensures public trust through adherence to accuracy, fairness, and impartiality, which is essential for credible reporting (McBride & Rosenstiel,2013). This code guides decision-making in complex scenarios, protects journalistic integrity against bias and external pressures, and demands accountability through transparent reporting and necessary corrections. It also upholds press freedom, supports public interest, and emphasizes journalism's role as a democratic watchdog (Janowitz, 2018). By enhancing professionalism, a code of ethics sets journalism apart as a disciplined quest for truth, promoting a responsible and ethical media landscape (Encabo, 1995).

In mainland China, the Professional Ethics Code requires respect for news subjects' rights, protection of vulnerable groups, and strict compliance with legal reporting standards to maintain judicial integrity. However, it lacks comprehensive guidance on conducting interviews, handling sources, and writing stories in a way that protects victims and regulates reporting on sensitive issues like sexual violence. Journalists I interviewed often expressed confusion about achieving balanced reporting or whether to side with victims, which can lead to the news media being judged before trial (Xinhua, 2019).

In Hong Kong, ethical codes fail to specify how to report sexual violence, leaving gaps that could result in secondary victimization. For instance, excessive detail in reports can cause discomfort to the public and additional harm to the individuals involved, as seen in campus sexual harassment coverage.

Taiwan is recognized for its effectiveness in this field. On August 11, 2024, the Ministry of Health and Welfare Department issued guidelines for media reporting on incidents involving minors and sexual violence. These guidelines strictly prohibit revealing victims' identities and also accused individuals who are minors or the relatives and partners of victims. The guideline also provides detailed advice on journalistic practices, including avoiding invasive interviewing and filming techniques to avoid second harm to the victims, withholding judgment before trial, and omitting graphic descriptions of sexual assault (Ministry of Health and Welfare, 2024). Of course, these are recommendations, and their adherence depends on media outlets implementing more specific internal regulations, such as banning certain explicit content in reports, which, although attention-grabbing, can be damaging. However, the government guidance provides a detailed framework for news outlets to detail the operational practices.

Legal Support

When reporting on cases of sexual violence, news media and journalists frequently encounter legal challenges stemming from allegations made by victims. "I put too much trust in the victim and did not ask for additional evidence. As a result, I lost the case." Taiwanese journalist J6 shared his experience of being sued after he reported on a sexual assault allegation. The lawsuit resulted in a court-mandated compensation payment. Fortunately, his employer provided comprehensive legal support, covering everything from attorney fees to the payment of damages. However, not all journalists are fortunate enough to receive such extensive legal backing from their employers—some are unwilling to bear the costs. In contrast, others lack the financial resources to handle legal expenses.

Lawsuits significantly chill journalists, inhibiting their freedom of expression and impacting democratic engagement (Reese & Shoemaker, 2018; Shoemaker, 1996). They can impose immense psychological and financial pressure on journalists, leading to self-censorship and reduced aggressive investigative reporting (Townend, 2017). This chilling effect extends beyond individual journalists to the broader public, who are deprived of critical information, thereby undermining democracy and public participation. Consequently, news organizations are responsible for providing legal support to journalists.

Industry associations and social organizations can also offer legal assistance to journalists as a crucial supplement. For example, although the amounts are small, the Hong Kong Journalists Association (HKJA) provides its members with legal aid and offers legal services to online media. In Taiwan, the Journalists Association, through its team of lawyers, protects the legal rights of its members and assists them in advocating for press freedom and independence. This reflects the importance of journalistic professional organizations; however, in Hong Kong, the HKJA is constantly under the government's security, especially from Beijing, which raises the concern of how journalists can be better protected without this kind of organization.

In mainland China, the Journalists' Association, part of the government apparatus, does not provide legal aid services. However, since the state owns the news media, individuals typically do not target these media over sensitive issues like sexual violence. Despite limited reporting on such incidents by these media, victims often seek justice through public opinion on social media, where citizen journalists bear the responsibility and constantly face legal challenges. In such cases, legal assistance from social organizations is incredibly crucial, and currently, some lawyers are stepping forward voluntarily to take on this responsibility; however, this creates the issue of whether this help would be sustained.

Mental Health Support

Reporting on sexual violence involves not only protecting the victims from secondary harm but also considering the mental health of journalists, who act as both listeners and reporters. During interviews, many journalists have admitted to feeling significant psychological pressure after covering such cases. Mainland journalist J14 shared that after interviewing several underage girls who were forced into prostitution following rape, he felt deeply depressed for an extended period.

> During that time, I sometimes felt out of control. I pretended to be calm, yet I could not stay calm. I even had nightmares about unfamiliar girls crying. Although I tried hard to complete my assigned interviews, my colleagues and friends later told me I was restless during that period. I did not understand why then, but now I think it was because I had heard and seen too much, especially those young girls. It was hard to accept that such things could happen.

Another mainland journalist, J12, described his feelings upon discovering that the person accused in a sexual harassment case he was assigned to cover was someone he knew:

> It was shocking and unbelievable because it was so unlike the person I knew. I could not accept it because I always thought he was a good person. I asked my editor to be excused from covering this news because I was supposed to interview the accused for his response, but I did not know how to approach him. To this day, I avoid him and have never met him face-to-face.

Hong Kong journalist J22 recounted receiving persistent text messages from the accused after the report was published:

> I gave the accused a chance to respond, which was necessary if they were willing to speak. However, the accused was unhappy with my report but did not say so directly. Instead, he continually texted me about how my report had changed his life. I did not block him because I did not feel it was necessary, as I thought I could handle it. However, looking back, it was not the case. Every time I saw his messages, my mood for the day would deteriorate, making it difficult to speak calmly with people around me.

Taiwanese journalist J6, after covering several cases of sexual violence, proactively requested his supervisor to exempt him from interviewing victims: "Even if I had contacted the victims, I would still avoid them. I told my boss I would handle the legal aspects because they are more detached, allowing me to separate myself from my deep sympathy for the victims."

The importance of providing mental health support for journalists is underscored by the challenges faced by female journalists, who encounter both external and internal sexual harassment. Findings from surveys and interviews show that journalists on the front lines in Hong Kong face not just physical injuries, including permanent disabilities, but also psychological distress that may impact their long-term health and encourage self-censorship. Female journalists are particularly vulnerable, facing discrimination that affects their career opportunities due to benevolent sexist attitudes from editors and news consumers, resulting in fewer assignments to cover frontline protests, which are often seen as "man's work." With 87% of survey participants agreeing on the need for news organizations to offer counseling for journalists who endure violence while covering protests, this study and others highlight the urgent need for more research into the mental health challenges faced by journalists in such environments (Luqiu, 2022).

While journalists in Hong Kong face external sexual harassment due to their profession, journalists in mainland China and Taiwan confront sexual harassment within the newsroom. A survey among female journalists in mainland China revealed a severe situation that requires attention. In 2021, a notable case linked to the #MeToo movement involved former journalist He Qian, who accused her supervisor, Deng Fei, at *Phoenix Weekly*. Deng won a libel case against He, setting back the movement in China (Hernandez, 2021). Without serious and systematic efforts to address these issues, sexual harassment will persist, similar to other sectors like higher education. In Taiwan, while exact figures on sexual harassment in news organizations are not available, several cases involving senior media management were exposed by social media during the 2023 #MeToo wave. An interviewee from this study shared their experience with an internal sexual harassment case and expressed dissatisfaction with the newsroom management's handling of the situation, leading to confusion, unhappiness, and, ultimately, resignation.

Offering mental support to journalists is crucial, especially in light of findings from studies that have explored the emotional health impacts faced by those in the media industry. Research has clearly shown that journalists who are subjected to intimidation and harassment during their professional duties may develop various levels of post-traumatic stress (Backholm & Björkqvist, 2010; Feinstein, 2012). This condition not only affects their immediate psychological health but can also have long-term repercussions on their overall well-being and ability to function effectively in high-pressure environments. The newsroom's and its management's role in addressing these issues is paramount. A newsroom that provides support and a sympathetic understanding of journalists' mental health challenges correlates strongly with higher job satisfaction and morale. More importantly, such support is linked with a sustained desire among journalists to continue in their roles within the media industry (Beam & Spratt, 2009). This relationship indicates that journalists' environment is as critical as their external challenges.

Providing mental health support can take various forms, such as offering access to psychological counseling, creating peer support groups, and establishing protocols that minimize exposure to traumatic situations without compromising journalistic duty. Additionally, training for managers and editors to recognize symptoms of stress and trauma can enable quicker interventions, potentially mitigating the severity of emotional responses. These studies underscore that mental health support is not just a personal benefit but a professional necessity that can determine the quality and integrity of journalism. Ensuring that journalists have access to the necessary emotional and psychological resources is essential for maintaining a resilient and effective media workforce capable of performing its critical role in society.

Several Chinese online resources are available for mental health support tailored to journalists, such as those offered on the website of *Reporters Without Borders*. These resources guide emotional and mental health management specifically designed for journalists. While these online materials are beneficial, more is needed to fully meet the needs of journalists who often face unique and severe stressors. In regions like Hong Kong, some NGOs offer workshops tailored to journalists, focusing on practical skills for managing stress and trauma encountered in the field. Similarly, in Taiwan, media outlets like *The Reporter* have begun to include counseling services as part of their medical benefits for journalists. This is a positive step, but more comprehensive and sustainable mechanisms are needed within news organizations.

News organizations should consider integrating mental health services directly into their health benefits packages to build a sustainable support system. By institutionalizing counseling services and making them a standard part of health insurance, newsrooms can ensure consistent and reliable access to mental health support. This approach not only benefits the journalists by providing immediate and ongoing support but also enhances the overall resilience and productivity of the newsroom. For long-term, such institutional support can help maintain high professional standards and morale, significantly impacting the quality and depth of journalism produced. This strategic investment in journalists' well-being is essential for fostering a healthy, sustainable work environment facing modern reporting challenges.

Mandatory Gender Studies in Journalism Education

An examination of the journalism bachelor's programs at three public universities in Hong Kong—the University of Hong Kong, Chinese University of Hong Kong, and Hong Kong Baptist University—reveals that none of these institutions have a dedicated gender studies course within their curriculum. The same observation applies to Taiwan's National Chengchi University, Shih Hsin University, Fu Jen Catholic University, Mainland China's Fudan University, Renmin University, and Communication University of China. While undergraduate students can opt to take gender-related courses offered by other departments, the lack of specialized gender courses within journalism programs is notable. For instance, I teach a general education course on gender at Hong Kong Baptist University, and for each semester, a few journalism students choose to enroll. However, I cannot focus on journalism because it is a GE course. I have to use storytelling to accommodate non-journalism students. The principles and techniques for storytelling are different from news reporting. The lack of tailor-made gender courses for journalism schools raises a critical question: Should they incorporate specific gender courses into their curricula? Moreover, how do we implement these courses?

There are some effects in other countries. North's (2010) research reveals a significant gap in Australian undergraduate journalism education concerning gender issues. The study scrutinized undergraduate journalism courses across 30 Australian universities and found that none of these programs offered a specific unit dedicated to exploring the portrayal of women in media, the gendered production of news, or the gender dynamics within newsrooms. This absence highlights the neglect of gender education in journalism despite its critical role in addressing systemic inequities faced by women in media organizations. Five years later, North (2015) reported on positive developments by introducing the first unit in an Australian journalism program that addresses the gendered nature of news content and production processes. This unit pioneered to tackle entrenched industry biases and included core content that sparked student and institutional engagement. Despite its success, the paper pointed out ongoing challenges in expanding such modules across other programs, emphasizing the need for broader adoption of gender and diversity education within journalism curricula to combat the industry's deep-seated biases and foster a more inclusive media landscape.

Incorporating gender issues into journalism curricula presents significant challenges. Bamezai et al. (2020) investigates the impact and effectiveness of gender mainstreaming (GM) in journalism education across 34 journalism schools in India, spanning both public and private institutions. The study reveals that although there is an awareness of gender issues, the implementation of GM is irregular and fragmented. Gender-related content often needs to be more cohesive within specific topics or papers, which limits its impact on broader educational practices, content interpretation, and diversity in research topics. Despite increasing female enrollment in journalism courses, this has not led to proportional representation in the media industry or decreased gender discrimination and attrition rates among women. The study underscores the need for a more substantial commitment to GM in journalism education, which could lead to affirmative policies that significantly alter media discourse around the exploitation, disempowerment, and marginalization of women, thus addressing fundamental issues of gender discrimination and violence within the industry. The research by Larrondo and Rivero (2019) examines the integration of gender issues into journalism education at Spanish universities, both public and private. Through content analysis and qualitative questionnaires aimed at academic staff, the findings indicate that gender equality is not yet a core component of teaching and learning strategies in Spanish journalism programs. Although significant curriculum reforms have been initiated to create a more gender-aware educational environment, the actual integration of a gender perspective largely depends on the individual initiative of faculty members, contrasting with broader institutional efforts to promote gender parity in other university operations. The results suggest that while there is a movement toward a more gender-inclusive approach in higher education, the systemic integration of gender issues into journalism studies remains limited and reliant on the commitment of individual educators to these principles.

U.S. journalism schools face significant challenges regarding gender representation in educational materials, mainly textbooks. Studies, such as those analyzing sports journalism textbooks, reveal a stark male predominance in content depiction, with men highlighted much more frequently than women. This imbalance extends to general journalism textbooks, which often portray the profession through a masculine lens, mainly after women started entering the field in more significant numbers during World War II, seemingly to deter their permanent inclusion post-war. Even with the advent of Open Educational Resources (OER) and discussions aimed at increasing diversity, educational practices often continue to replicate these gendered biases, calling into question the effectiveness of current efforts to make journalism education more inclusive. This ongoing issue suggests that journalism education in the United States is still far from providing an equitable learning environment, particularly for female students, thereby perpetuating historical gender biases within the profession (Colgan, 2017; Hardin et al., 2006; Heckman & Homan, 2020).

Portugal is a positive example, demonstrating that international cooperation is an effective strategy to boost motivation in addressing gender issues in journalism. The formal undergraduate journalism curricula in Portugal have not traditionally focused on how gender influences news content and production. However, since 2005, the University of Coimbra has provided non-formal educational opportunities through its involvement with the Global Media Monitoring Project (GMMP). Coordinated by the Faculty of Arts and Humanities, this initiative has engaged numerous students in activities aimed at mainstreaming gender in media-related policies to address inequalities and combat discriminatory norms against women. A recent study employing an ethnographic approach, including participant observations, underscores the success of these GMMP activities. It highlights the positive impact on students and calls for a more formal integration of gender topics into journalism education based on compelling student experiences and feedback in preparation for the 2020 edition of the GMMP (Simões et al., 2021).

The pervasive influence of media on society underscores the critical need for mandatory gender courses in journalism schools to promote gender equality and shape societal norms. Feminist media scholars emphasize that equal access to public discourse and fair representation in media are as crucial for achieving gender equality as access to health, education, and political decision-making. Persistent issues in journalism, such as unbalanced representation, gender stereotyping, and the predominance of male voices, along with systemic problems like limited access for women in decision-making roles, pay inequality, and a predominantly masculine culture in newsrooms, underscore the profound societal implications of gender inequality in the field (North, 2015). Gender education in journalism is crucial because the media significantly perpetuates or challenges social norms and values. Integrating comprehensive gender studies into journalism curricula equips future media professionals with the tools to foster a more inclusive and equitable media environment. This education goes beyond simply altering content; it aims to transform the environment in which news is created. Courses on gender could explore critical areas such as reporting on issues like sexual violence, understanding the impact of gender bias in media portrayal, and developing strategies for more equitable coverage. In addition to changing the way stories are told, gender education in journalism could lead to more profound changes within newsrooms. Changing these spaces' culture requires everyone, from journalists to editors and management, to develop a keen awareness of gender issues. This awareness should be grounded in personal experiences and a robust educational foundation in gender studies. Such education is crucial for fostering an inclusive and sensitized media environment to the nuances of gender issues. This approach can fundamentally shift how stories are framed, reported, and understood, contributing to a more informed and equitable public discourse. Ultimately, including gender studies in journalism education is a strategic move toward reshaping the media landscape to reflect and respect the diverse society it serves. By doing so, journalism can fulfill its role as a pillar of democracy and an agent of social change, ensuring that all voices are heard and represented fairly in the media.

In societies with Chinese language contexts, such as Hong Kong, mainland China, and Taiwan, the importance of integrating gender studies into journalism education is particularly pronounced. These societies often grapple with deep-rooted cultural norms and historical values that can perpetuate gender stereotypes and hinder gender equality in media representation. The Confucian ideals emphasizing hierarchy and patriarchy can still influence contemporary social and media narratives, often sidelining discussions about gender equality and women's rights. Implementing gender studies in journalism curricula within these contexts demands culturally sensitive approaches that consider local social norms while challenging regressive stereotypes. Initiatives could include partnerships with gender-focused NGOs to provide real-world case studies, guest lectures by scholars specializing in gender and media within Chinese societies, and the development of case studies that reflect local and regional issues. Furthermore, encouraging student-led media projects that focus on gender issues can help cultivate a new generation of journalists who are aware of and actively involved in reshaping the discourse around gender in their societies.

To effectively implement gender studies within journalism curricula in Chinese-speaking societies, a strategic approach centered on curriculum reform is essential. This reform should involve collaboration between gender studies scholars and journalism educators to design tailor-made courses that interweave feminist theories with journalistic practice. These courses should comprehensively address gender issues, including, but not limited to, reporting on sexual violence and LGBTQ+ issues. The curriculum should be crafted to provide a balanced integration of theoretical understanding and practical application. Courses could start with foundational feminist theories and then move into specific journalistic practices that challenge and refine these theories through media production. Practical modules might include workshops on sensitive reporting techniques for sexual violence and fair coverage of LGBTQ+ matters, ensuring students learn about these issues and apply their knowledge in real-world journalistic contexts. Additionally, the curriculum could benefit from including case studies and examples specific to the Chinese cultural context, helping students understand and navigate the unique challenges of traditional societal norms. By prioritizing this comprehensive, culturally informed, and practice-oriented approach, journalism schools can create a dynamic learning environment that equips future journalists with the tools to foster a more inclusive and equitable media landscape in Chinese-speaking regions.

References

Backholm, K., & Björkqvist, K. (2010). The effects of exposure to crisis on well-being of journalists: A study of crisis-related factors predicting psychological health in a sample of Finnish journalists. *Media, War & Conflict*, *3*(2), 138–151.

Bamezai, G., Roy, A., Roy, A., & Chhetri, S. (2020). Gender mainstreaming as an essential part of journalism education in India. *World of Media. Journal of Russian Media and Journalism Studies*, (3), 1–33.

Beam, R. A., & Spratt, M. (2009). Managing vulnerability: Job satisfaction, morale and journalists' reactions to violence and trauma. *Journalism Practice*, *3*(4), 421–438.

Colgan, J. (2017). Gender bias in international relations graduate education? New evidence from syllabi. *PS: Political Science & Politics*, *50*(2), 456–460.

Cuklanz, L. (2020). Problematic news framing of# MeToo. *The Communication Review*, *23*(4), 251–272.

Encabo, M. N. (1995). The ethics of journalism and democracy. *European Journal of Communication*, *10*(4), 513–526.

Feinstein, A. (2012). Mexican journalists: An investigation of their emotional health. *Journal of Traumatic Stress*, *25*(4), 480–483.

Hardin, M., Dodd, J. E., & Lauffer, K. (2006). Passing it on: The reinforcement of male hegemony in sports journalism textbooks. *Mass Communication & Society*, *9*(4), 429–446.

Heckman, M. (2023). Constructing the "gender beat:" US journalists refocus the news in the aftermath of# Metoo. *Journalism Practice*, *17*(7), 1413–1427.

Heckman, M., & Homan, M. (2020). The syllabus is a boys' club: The paucity of woman authors in journalism course materials. *Teaching Journalism & Mass Communication*, *10*(2), 15–21.

Hernandez, A. C. (2021). She said #MeToo. Now she's being punished under defamation law. *The New York Times.* Retrieved from https://www.nytimes.com/2021/01/08/world/asia/china-metoo-defamation.html

Janowitz, M. (2018). Professional models in journalism: The gatekeeper and the advocate. In Margaret Scammell, Holli Semetko. *The Media, Journalism and Democracy* (pp. 109–118). Routledge.

Kim, K. H., & Yoon, Y. (2009). The influence of journalists' gender on newspaper stories about women Cabinet members in South Korea. *Asian Journal of Communication, 19*(3), 289–301.

Lai, C. (2018). Over 80% of female journalists in China have experienced workplace sexual harassment, poll by journalist shows. Hong Kong Free Press. Retrieved from https://hongkongfp.com/2018/03/07/80-female-journalists-china-experienced-workplace-sexual-harassment-poll-journalist-shows/

Larrondo, A., & Rivero, D. (2019). A case study on the incorporation of gender-awareness into the university journalism curriculum in Spain. *Gender and Education, 31*(1), 1–14.

Luqiu, L. R. (2022). Female journalists covering the Hong Kong protests confront ambivalent sexism on the street and in the newsroom. *Feminist Media Studies, 22*(3), 679–697.

McBride, K., & Rosenstiel, T. (Eds.). (2013). *The new ethics of journalism: Principles for the 21st century.* CQ Press.

Ministry of Health and Welfare. (2024). Guidelines for media reporting on incidents involving minors and sexual violence. Retrieved from https://dep.mohw.gov.tw/dops/fp-1287-79602-105.html

North, L. (2010). The gender 'problem' in Australian journalism education. *Australian Journalism Review, 32*(2), 103–115.

North, L. (2015). The currency of gender: Student and institutional responses to the first gender unit in an Australian journalism program. *Journalism & Mass Communication Educator, 70*(2), 174–186.

Reese, S. D., & Shoemaker, P. J. (2018). A media sociology for the networked public sphere: The hierarchy of influences model. In Ran Wei *Advances in Foundational Mass Communication Theories* (pp. 96–117). Routledge.

Shoemaker, P. J. (1996). Mediating the message: Theories of influences on mass media content.

Simões, R. B., Amaral, I., & Santos, S. (2021). Gender and journalism education: Undergraduate students responses to the Global Media Monitoring Project. In *INTED2021 Proceedings* (pp. 6095–6099). IATED.

Steiner, L. (2019). Gender, sex, and newsroom culture. In Karin Wahl-Jorgensen, Thomas Hanitzsch *The handbook of journalism studies* (pp. 452–468). Routledge.

Townend, J. (2017). Freedom of expression and the chilling effect. In Howard Tumber, Silvio Waisbord. *The Routledge companion to media and human rights* (pp. 73–82). Routledge.

Trussardi, L. (2022). Are journalists aware of the gender gap?: A study on the perceptions and experiences about the language used in the representation of women in the Italian press.

Xinhua. (2019). The professional ethics code for Chinese news workers. Retrieved from https://www.xinhuanet.com/politics/2019-12/15/c_1125348618.htm

Zhang, P., & Guo, R. (2011). Crazy English founder Li Yang accused of domestic abuse against his daughter by his former wife Kim Lee. *South China Moring Post.* Retrieved from https://www.scmp.com/news/people-culture/china-personalities/article/3146866/crazy-english-founder-li-yang-accused

Index

Note: *Italic* page numbers refer to figures.

For Product Safety Concerns and Information please contact our EU representative GPSR@taylorandfrancis.com
Taylor & Francis Verlag GmbH, Kaufingerstraße 24, 80331 München, Germany

www.ingramcontent.com/pod-product-compliance
Lightning Source LLC
LaVergne TN
LVHW010937110826
845149LV00013B/2644

* 9 7 8 1 0 3 2 7 5 5 6 8 7 *